'... Before the Devil Knows You're Dead'

Irish Blessings, Toasts and Curses

'... Before the Devil Knows You're Dead'

Irish Blessings, Toasts and Curses

Padraic O'Farrell

MERCIER PRESS

Mercier Press
PO Box 5, 5 French Church Street, Cork
16 Hume Street, Dublin 2

ISBN 1 85635 033 9

A CIP is available of this book from the British Library.

10 9 8 7 6 5 4 3 2

To Jessica

I have made every attempt to ensure that copyright material is not printed without permission. The origin of some material is so obscure that it is impossible to be certain that I have covered all the ground. However if inadvertent use is noted I would be grateful for having my attention drawn to it and I hope this note will be taken as an apology.

Printed in Ireland by Colour Books Ltd.

Contents

Blessings

Toasts and Hearty Wishes

Curses

General Blessings

As we become good Europeans and embrace all the implications, good or evil, of that status, it is difficult to realise that not so many years ago, little of our everyday business was undertaken without the benefit of God's blessing invoked by ourselves or others. Going to fish or save turf, hearing news of a death or marriage, consoling neighbours in sorrow or sharing their joy – there was a particular blessing for every occasion and people uttered these ejaculations without fear of being considered passé or over-religious. Some of these habits have survived. The simple 'God bless you', 'God save you', or 'God rest his soul' are heard as often as they are mocked, at least.

Many of the following blessings are translated from the Irish; others are remembered from a rural childhood. All have their own charm.

Animals, Birds etc.

'Oh that God Almighty may bless us and save us,' says I;
'That's a good word ye said,' said the little grey horse.

The blessing of Mary, the blessing of God
The blessing of sun, moon and road;
Of man from the east, of man from the west,
My blessing on you – be you blest.
(Said when milking.)

May the holes in your nets be no larger than the fish in it.

May you be Christ's ghillie and the trout leppin'.

May you have a fast slip and a long course.

God bless three times with three spits for luck.
(Said at the birth of livestock.)

7

God bless you, cow
May He double bless your calf.
Come, Mary and sit,
Come Brigid and milk,
Come, Blessed Michael the Archangel
And bless this fat beast
In the name of the Father and of the Son and of the Holy
    Ghost.
(From the Irish.)

Hurs slán agus Dia leat.
*(Hurs health and God be with you. Said by farming women as they
caught the cow's tail at milking time. 'Hurs' was a common cow-call.)*

Here's to the grey goose
With the golden wing;
A free country
And a Fenian king.
(IFC Ms, Vol, 583, p.276.)

May the loss of Aughrim be your only loss.
(Small loss.)

May there be a fox on your fishing-hook, and a hare on your
bait.

Death

May I never kill a person and may nobody kill me. But if
someone thinks of killing me, may I kill him.
(From the Irish.)

Ar dheas Dé go raibh a anam.
(May his soul be on the right hand of God.)

The Lord have mercy on his soul (or) God's free mercy be on his soul.

God's blessing be on the souls of the dead and may we be a long time following them.

May God grant you a generous share of eternity.

That you may never be left to die a sinner.

> May we see God's countenance
> And perceive His gloriousness.
> And attain His paradise.
> > A death of blessedness,
> > Penance and clemency
> > May our poor souls have.

(Douglas Hyde.)

> Blessed Virgin, God's own mother,
> Shining light set up on high,
> Candle blazing in the heavens, be with me the day I die.

(Ibid.)

May the grass on the road to hell grow long.

> Oh Brigid, Mary of the Gael,
> Oh Brigid, extend your aid;
> Keep me under your protection from all harm
> Until I die in the companionship of God.

> Blessed Mary, queen of grace
> Look after my soul every hour of each day.
> When it passes beyond my cold, weak body

Grant it succour on its way.
(From the Irish.)

To Christ the seed
To Christ the harvest
In God's haggard
May we meet.
(From the Irish.)

May you see Him in heaven.

May heaven be your bed.

May God level the road for his soul.

May you have a smith's *meitheal* at your wake.
(A big crowd.)

The Lord be good to you on Judgement Day.

When you reach the inn of death, I hope it's closing time.

No black stick when you reach Lúibín na gCorp.
(A spot where coffins were laid down and opened during a funeral; if the corpse had been removed by the sídhe, a black stick was placed inside instead.)

May there be rain at your funeral.
(Considered a good omen.)

May St Michael have a blast in his eye and the Devil without ballast on your Judgement Day.
(St Michael was said to weigh good deeds, the devil bad ones.)

Solus Mhich Dé chuig a n-anam.
(The light of the Son of God on her soul.)

May you receive mercy and grace; death without sin; and
may the righteous gone before you receive their share of
eternal glory.
(From the Irish.)

May you and yours be farthest from the grave.

On your deathbed, may you have the grace of God and of
your neighbours.

Health and Welfare

God's bounty to you and your stock.

> God for the good day,
> God for the bad day,
> God for the pleasure,
> God for the pain,
> God for the rain,
> God when our barns are empty,
> God when they're full again.

(Said during food shortage. IFC Ms, Vol 578, p.255.)

May you never bear the heavy load of an empty stomach.

Saol fada agus breac-shláinte chugat.
(Long life and middling health to you.)

> May white snuff be at your wake,
> Bakers bread and curran-y cake

And plinty on your table, late and soon.
(John B. Keane, Sive, Act 1, Scene 3.)

Bless us, Lord
Bless our food and our drink
And you who bought us dearly
Save us from all evil.
(From the Irish.)

May you only grow old in the face
Be treasured and cared for with grace.

Mary and her son, Brigid and her cloak, God and His strength between you and pestilence.
(Or some named disease.)

Praise be to the mother in the Garden of Paradise
Once without fault.
O only son of Mary and King of Grace,
Do not let the poor soul stray.
(From the Irish.)

Bless you and your clan and may every limb of your body be as strong as the Fianna's stick.
(From the Irish.)

God grant you health and happiness, old stock!

May God speak kindly to you.

God and John the Baptist give you long life and happiness.

May you have rye bread to do you good,
Wheaten bread to sweeten your blood,

12

Barley bread to do you no harm
And oatmeal bread to strengthen your arm.

May your *poll an phaidrín* (hole near chimney where rosary beads and other bric-a-brac were kept) never be empty.

My thousand blessings and God's blessing on you and may you never want for anything.

The face of life and health and the beating of all be yours.

Christ walked on the rock
A horse's foot was injured.
He put blood to blood,
Flesh to flesh,
Bone to bone.
As he cured that,
May he cure this.
(From the Irish.)

Christ of the wounds, crucified on the tree, preserve your health.

God bless the mark.
(Said upon noticing some defect or disability.)

With the help of God, you'll pull through.

May you always have food, clothing and a pillow for your head.

Seven times the full of St Patrick's graveyard,
Seven times the full of the tomb of Christ,

Seven times the full of the well of grace,
Of blessings on you until we see each other again.

The Lord have mercy on the souls of the dead.
(A cure for toothache if whispered to the patient.)

Bright glorious May
And my thousand blessings to you;
The best doctor's medicine to you
In sickness or in health.

May you escape the gallows, avoid distress, and be as
healthy as a trout.

God save you, my three brothers! God save you! How far
    have you to go?
To Mount Olivet, for gold for a cup to hold the tears of
    Christ.
Then go! Collect the gold, and may Christ's tears fall on it
    and you will be cured in body and in soul.
(From the Irish. Said while giving a drink to a person with a stitch in his side.)

The five loaves and the two fishes of the five thousand be
with God's people always.

My best, biggest and flouriest potatoes to you.

That your stirabout may always go 'puff puff' and never
'clip clap'.
(May it not be watery, i.e. May you have plenty.)

May springtime never be far away for you.

14

May I see you grey and your clan sensible.

Peace on your hand and health to all who shake it.

Whatever takes longest to come to you, may it be worth waiting for.

> A charm set by Mary for her son
> In the doorway of Christ's city,
> Against pain and headache
> May Jesus Christ banish from us
> The worm in the flesh,
> Which is harming the tooth
> And kill it!
> *(Seán O'Sullivan.)*

> May your barn be always full
> Free from fox and crow and gull.

May you have small potatoes for Old Nick, big floury ones for God and none for ...

> Jesus, Mary and Saint Joseph, I place you between me
>   and illness of the mind.
> I salute you, O green-leafed Tree,
> I salute you, O four-armed Cross,
> May no harm from this body before me
> Affect me.
> *(Said on entering a wake-house, to prevent infection. Seán O'Sullivan.)*

May big headaches and little fevers stay far from you always.

Sláinte an bhradáin agat.
(Health of the salmon to you.)

The strength of St Patrick's horse to you.

Sláinte na bromaí agat.
(The strength of the colt to you.)

Long life and salvation to you, may you stay alive, healthy
and protected from harm.

May you live as long as you want and never want as long as
you live.

God between us and all harm.
(Also used in sympathy about another's misfortune.)

May you have a long life and a quiet life, and good health
with it.
(J.M. Synge, The Shadow of the Glen, *Finale.)*

That you may never comb a grey head.

May you have health to wear it.
(Said on seeing a new garment being worn.)

A blessing will not fill the stomach but take it anyhow.

May I see you grey and combing your children's hair.

> The Lord rade and the foal slade,
> He lighted and He righted;

Set joint to joint and bone to bone
And sinew unto sinew.
In the name of God and the Saints,
Of Mary and her son,
Let this man be healed.
(Uttered while wool is wound around a sprained ankle. Lady Wilde.)

May Peter take, may Paul take, may Michael take, the pain away, the cruel pain that kills the back and the life, and darkens the eyes.
(Ibid. Written on paper which is tied to a hare's foot to be worn by someone suffering from pain.)

God spare you the years to smoke your dudeen, drink your cruiskeen, flourish your alpeen to wallop a spalpeen.

Nár laga Dia thú
(May God not weaken you.)

Go maire tú
(May you live.)

God rest Paul's soul.
(Said when passing between a patient and the fire to prevent catching the disease.)

Never a *guí gann* in your life.
(Scarce blessing. A prayer only for friends.)

To the doctor may you never hand any money,
And sweet be your hand in a pot full of honey.

May you never be like Biddy Maher with her little skillet.

The health of the risen to you.

May there never be a rattle in your skillet.

May you never see the bottom of your pot.

That your griddle may always be hot.

May you never be beyond cutting a flitch.

That the face of all good news and the back of all bad news be towards you.

May you have a gentleman for a landlord.

May God give you your share of food and the Host as long as you live and your family after that.

That God may give you the back to bear the burden.

More power to your elbow.

May the strength of three be in your journey through life.

God bless you and keep you, mother machree.

May you never see a poor day.

The Lord keep you in his hand but never close his fist too tight on you.

God's help be always nearer than the door for you.

There was a large boiler in the Sligo's workhouse yard during the Famine and another on the site of the present courthouse. Ejaculations of starving people struggling towards these locations were noted; few of them expressed bitterness:

'Welcome be the will of God.'
'May God increase your store for your kindness to one more needy than yourself.'
'May God give you a bed in heaven.'
'May the blessing of God be about you.'
'May God bless you and yours.'
'May the Lord have mercy on the souls of your departed friends.'
'God's ways are not our ways.'
'May the Light of Heaven shine on you.'
'Glory, honour and thanks to God for everything.'
'Thanks be to God.'
(IFC Ms, Vol. 485, p. 244.)

Glory be to God on high
Only for the bit we ate we'd die!
Prayer and fasting are good for a sinner
But a hungry man would want his dinner.

God save you Archangel Michael! God save you!
What ails you, man?
A headache, an ailment and a heart weakness,
Archangel Michael; can you cure me angel of the Lord?
May three things cure you, man:
May the shadow of Christ fall on you;
May the garment of Christ swathe you;
May the breath of Christ breathe on you.
And when I call on you again you will be cured.
(Said over a patient while sprinkling water on his head as his arms are raised to a cruciform.)

Light in your eyes,
Teeth in your mouth,
Thatch on top.
Flesh on you,
Bone on you,
Legs and feet under you,
And a tail behind to guide you.

God keep you (alive).

The look of Mary, the look of God be on this blast.
(Said to someone with a sore eye.)

The look of Mary, the look of God take this headache away.
(Said to someone with a headache.)

Home

God bless the corners of this house
And be the lintel blessed.
Bless the hearth, the table too
And bless each place of rest.
Bless each door that opens wide
To stranger, kith and kin;
Bless each shining window-pane
That lets the sunshine in.
Bless the roof-tree up above
Bless every solid wall.
The peace of man, the peace of love,
The peace of God on all.
(Featured on pictures that hung in kitchens many years ago. Origin unknown.)

Bless my humble kitchen, Lord,
I love its every nook.

Bless me as I toil in it
About my daily work.
Bless the meals that I prepare
Grant seas'ning from above.
Bestow Thy blessing and Thy grace
And most of all, your love.
As we prepare to eat our meal
May you the table spread,
Let us not forget to thank you, Lord
For all our daily bread.
So bless my humble kitchen, Lord,
And all who enter it;
Bless them with joy and peace and love
As happily they sit.
(Ditto.)

May the blessing of the five loaves and two fishes that God divided among five thousand be ours and may the King who divided place pot luck in our food and in our portion.
(Said before meals.)

The luck of God, the prosperity of Patrick on all whom I see and on all whom I take. May God grant to this bread the luck he bestowed on the five loaves and two fishes.
(Said when kneading bread.)

I will light my fire today
In the presence of the holy angels of heaven
In the presence of the sweetly formed Airil
In the presence of the greatest beauty, Uiril,
Without hate, without envy, without rivalry.
Without fear, without dread of anyone under the sun
And the Holy Son of God my protector.
God, you kindle in my heart the ember of love
For my enemies, my friends and relations;
To the wise, the foolish, the slave,

21

O Son of Mary, gently bright.
From the lowest that could be picked
To the highest name.
(From the Irish.)

M'anam do Dhia agus do Mhuire.
(My soul to God and Mary. *Said after day's work*)

God bless all here.

The sweet protection of the three sons – the son of God, Mac Duagh and Mac Dara on all here.

I bank down this fire with the miraculous powers that
    Patrick got.
May the angels pile it, may no enemy pull it apart.
May God make a shelter of our house,
For all inside,
For all outside.
The sword of Christ over the door
Until the light of day tomorrow.
(From the Irish.)

May God sweep the dust of sin from our souls and from the souls of those close to Him.
(From the Irish. Said by poor servant girls.)

May your woman be a strong woman,
May your cows be white,
And may your house be on a height.
(Said to have been uttered by St Patrick who also used the reverse as a curse:

May your woman be an ugly woman,
May your cows be black beasts

And may your house be in a valley.
(Béaloideas, *Iml. V, Uimh.1, Meitheamh, 1935.*)

God guard this home from roof to floor
The Twelve Apostles guard the door;
Four good angels round each bed,
Two at the foot and two at the head.

King of the earth Who sent Christ from heaven,
Who sent Peter and Paul,
Destroy pests in blood and flesh when we go outside;
May the Father save us all and keep us safe from harm here
May they be blind, the hordes that might attack this home,
Christ keep all safe and wrap your protective cloak about us
    all.

Bless us, O Lord and these thy gifts which of Thy bounty we
are about to receive, through Christ Our Lord.
(Grace before meals.)

Mary, who with tender ward
Did keep the home of Christ the Lord,
And did set forth the bread and wine
Before the Living Wheat and Vine,
Please be beside me as I go
About my labours, to and fro',
Speed the wheel and speed the loom
And guide the needle and the broom.
Make my cakes rise sweet and light,
Cure my cheese a creamy white.
Yellow may my butter be
Like cowslips growing in the lea.
Guard my skillets big and small,
Fill them with good food for all.
Guide my needles and my wool,
Keep my larder safe and full.
To me your gracious help afford

23

Oh holy handmaid of the Lord.
(Assorted versions of the above known as 'The Housewife's Prayer'.)

Love and Marriage

O woman loved by me, may you give me your heart, your soul and your body.
(Said close by a mill-wheel, stream and tree as the man presents butter on a new plate to the girl.)

May you never be a blue bride, allanah.
(In the west of Ireland, a 'Shrove Tuesday bride' i.e. one who was pregnant and forced to marry, was called a blue bride.)

May your partner be his own man to the power of two.

May the king's evil be cured for you.
(Said as someone is blessed with water from a well near the Boyne river, where King James is said to have washed his sword after the battle.)

In the name of Mary and of St Patrick, archbishop of all of Ireland, may every evil be banished from everywhere.
(Uttered against king's evil and eczema. Seán O'Sullivan.)

May you sleep in your man's dirty nightshirt and not rue it.
(Such sleep was said to win the man's heart.)

That your love knot may be sealed with heaven's wax.

May luck be to the married couple.

Help and deliverance and friendship of God on you both.
God grant you a gradle of joy.
(Wedding blessing. Gradle means 'great deal'.)

Guím grásta ort.
(I wish grace on you.)

May your peltin' paper be a hundred pound note.
(Document of consent to marry from a priest.)

You for me and I for thee and never another. Your face
turned to mine and away from all others.
(Said secretly by a woman after offering a drink to her man.)

May the health that got you for us leave you healthy with us,
with the help of God and the light of his grace.
(Said by a couple when their child is born.)

> The blessing of the saints and angels
> The blessing of anyone else who knows us;
> And my own blessing, without stain, to you
> Until the Kingdom of Glory.

(From the Irish. Said at betrothal.)

By the power that Christ brought from heaven, may you
love me, woman. As the sun follows its course, may you
follow me. As light to the eye, as bread to the hungry, as joy
to the heart, may your presence be with me, woman that I
love, till death comes to part us asunder.

A golden ring on your swollen body.
(Said to a pregnant woman.)

O Christ, by your five wounds, by the nine orders of angels,
if this woman is ordained for me let me grasp her hand and
breathe her breath. *Mo grádh,* I place a talisman to your
crown, to the sole of your foot, to each of your breasts so that
you may never leave or forsake me. As the foal after the
mare, as the child after the mother, follow me and stay with

me until death do us part.

May you marry an orphan.
(i.e. you will never have trouble from in-laws.)

May you never marry a whistling woman.
(Regarded as evil.)

Go maire sibh bhur saol nua.
(Marriage congratulation: may you enjoy your new life.)

That your wife may knit for infants and may her needles
always click after dark.
(Such knitting was thought to be best, because sheep were asleep then.)

Mavourneen Dílis (my sweet darling) I offer you the love of
Christ for His Son down all our days.

> Come now listen while I sing
> To the blessing that I bring
> To the bridegroom and his lovely bride so fair.
> May they dwell in wedded joy
> May they ever hear the cry
> Of a new big bouncing baby every year.

(John B. Keane, Sive, Act 2, Scene 2.)

May your banns be read by a bishop.

May your bodies please each other like the stars do their
Master.

> The blessing that Mary placed on the butter
> The blessing for love and perpetual endearment:

That your body will not cease
Its awareness of mine;
That your love continues to follow my face
As the calf follows the cow
From this day to the day of my death.
(From the Irish.)

Oh, would it please the gods to split
Thy beauty, size, and years and wit,
No age could furnish out a pair
Of nymphs so graceful, wise and fair
With half the lustre of your eyes,
With half your wit, your years and size.
(Jonathan Swift, 'On Stella's Birthday'.)

May the man that you marry never have an old maid for a mother.

May your bed be soft and your man's hand along with it.

Sweet be her hand on you as if it came out of a pot of honey.

May your man never rise from an unfinished Mass, from food without offering grace or from yourself for another woman.

May your woman never burn her coal without heating herself.

May you never be sent to the gander paddock.
(Be in your wife's bad graces.)

Love, life and happiness; may your troubles be few and your blessings plenty.

Be there always a man's shirt on your clothes-line.

Sliocht sleachta ar shliocht bhur sleachta.
(May there be a generation of children on your children's children.)

Miscellaneous

May God and His saints protect you (until you return).

Musha, God give you sense.
(Said to somebody who sounds naive.)

May you never cross a stream in brown flood, a patch of soft grass or an angry woman.

May we see the bright light of tomorrow.

God bless the ground you walk upon.

May God give us food when we're hungry, money when we need it and heaven when we die.

If God sends you on a stony path, may he give you strong brogues (shoes).

God loves his own people; may they include you.

May God prepare you and Mary bless you.

May your voice be above every other voice,
That God may not strike down your care or your company.

Nollaig faoi shéan is faoi shonas duit.
(A prosperous and happy Christmas to you.)

May you never fear the will of God.

May peace and plenty be first to lift the latch of your door and happiness be guided to your home by the Christmas candle.

May your hand be stretched out in friendship but never in want during the coming year.
(A New Year blessing.)

> The Father in heaven
> And the Son who suffered the pain
> The Holy Ghost who strengthens us
> And the holy Virgin bless you in your trouble.

Go mbeirimid beo ar an am seo arís.
(May we all be alive this time next year. Said at Christmas meal and other annual celebrations.)

Go maire tú an lá.
(Many happy returns of the day.)

The blessing of Michael with his shield; of the palm branch of Christ, of Bridget with her veil on you.

The blessing of God's only Son who has purchased us dearly be on your trade.

God direct you in every task that lies ahead.

God prevent the evil eye from ever falling on you.

. Sand from heaven's shore in the eye of your enemy.

May your enemies never hear you.

God bless you; God buy you.

Good health to the bearer of good news and may bad news be far from you.

The sword of God defend you.

May you never see or hear what you hear or see or cut your throat with your tongue.

Go n-eírí an bóthar leat.
(Safe journey. Lit: May the road rise with you.)

May your path be convenient.

Go n-eírí an t-ádh leat.
(Good luck attend to you.)

The light of heaven to all things gone and may they never come back to haunt us.

May God increase your neighbours – those of them that are useful to you.
(From the Irish.)

God save all here bar the cat.
(Said upon entering a house. It was considered unlucky to bless the cat.)

30

God save Ireland.

The blessing of God on you.

Top of the morning to you.

God settle you and your trouble.

May you have a full moon on a dark night and the road downhill to your door.

May the wind be always at your back.

God between us and all harm.

Help and grace and friendship from God be on all here.

Ten thousand blessings upon all that's here ...
(John M. Synge, The Playboy of the Western World, *Finale.*)

Céad míle faílte romath.
(A hundred thousand welcomes to you.)

God keep you.

May the help of God be nearer than the door for you.

The light of heaven shine on you.

Take the world free and easy and may it take you the same.

If you have tears, may they turn God's mill-wheel.

May you have warm words on a cold evening.

May you be poor in misfortune, rich in blessings, slow to make enemies, fast to make friends; but rich or poor, slow or fast, may you know only happiness from this day out.

God bless you and your care (your family).

God guide you.

May God speak sweetly of you.

May God reward you.

May God tarry with you (or) God go with you always.

May God take you past the evil hour without loss or pain.

May you live till we see you again.

> May Christ and His saints come between you and harm.
> Mary and her Son;
> St Patrick with his staff;
> Martin with his mantle;
> Bridget with her veil;
> Michael with his shield
> And God over all with His strong right hand.
> *(Lady Wilde.)*

Heaven forbid that anything should happen to you.

> My hand and my word to you.

In the name of the victorious Father,
In the name of the Son who suffered pain,
In the name of the powerful Holy Ghost,
Let Mary and her Son join us on our journey.

May God be with you in victory.
You're the pick of the crowd,
You never flinched yet in a fray, my love.
May you beat the divil and every Cooleen.
(From the Irish. Urgings of the Black Mulvihill faction poet, Nancy Keane as quoted by Patrick O'Donnell.)

God bless the work.
(Answer: 'And you too.')

The hand of God rest lightly on you.

May you be seven times better throughout the year with support from the world, from health, and from the value of God's love and the goodness of people.
(From the Irish.)

May the eternal Father give you a share of the everlasting glory and health to those who labour and may God bring you safe from any danger that may come upon you.
(Uttered by those seeking alms.)

Self-Blessings

O countenance brighter than the sun, do not allow me to be long in pain.
(Douglas Hyde.)

    O King of Friday
    Whose limbs were stretched on the cross,
    O Lord who didst suffer
    The bruises, the wounds, the loss,
    We stretch ourselves
    Beneath the shield of Thy might,
    May some fruit from the tree of Thy passion
    Fall on us this night!
(Ibid.)

    The will of God be done by us,
    The law of God be kept by us,
    Our evil will controlled by us,
    Our tongue in cheek be held by us,
    Repentance timely made by us,
    Christ's passion understood by us,
    Each sinful crime be shunned by us,
    Much of the end be mused by us,
    And death be blessed found by us.
    With angels' music heard by us,
    And God's high praises sung to us
    For ever and for aye.
(Ibid.)

Health of the night's sleep to us.
(Ibid.)

God give me strength.

God forgive me.

I lie with God; may He lie with me.

May sin and loss be kept from me during the course of this day.

May I be kissed by all in red petticoats and check aprons between Kenmare and Killarney.

May I always meet my fetch at morning.
(Considered lucky.)

    Kindle inside my heart, O Lord
    The spark of love
    For my enemies, relatives and friends
(From the Irish.)

I see the moon, the moon sees me;
God bless the moon and God bless me.

    May Jesus be at my head,
    The Virgin at my feet
    The Twelve Apostles round my bed
    When I am fast asleep.

    There are four corners on my bed
    And over them four angels spread;
    Matthew, Mark, Luke and John
    God bless the bed that I lie on.
    If any evil comes to me,

O Holy Mary waken me
O God I give my soul to Thee.

Jesus this hour I give to Thee
For all the past hour pardon me.
I know that I shall soon depart
So hide me in Thy Sacred Heart.
(Said on the hour, every hour.)

Jesus the branch and Mary the flower
Jesus and Mary be with me all hours.

Christ be with me,
Christ inside me,
Christ behind me,
Christ in front of me,
Christ beside me,
Christ to win me,
Christ beneath me,
Christ above me,
Christ in peace,
Christ in danger,
Christ in the hearts of all who love me,
Christ in the mouths of all who hate me.
(Anonymous. From the Irish. Excerpt from The Lorica, *also known as* 'St
Patrick's Breastplate'.)

If I'm a bigger liar than the clock in Strabane itself, let me be
truthful to my friends.

God give me strength (to be patient).

Bless me, Lord, defend and govern me and after this short
and miserable pilgrimage bring me to everlasting life.

May the name of Jesus be firmly inscribed in the middle of my heart.

May God give me the nod to chance it like ...

Long eaters are long livers so let not my dinner be over before I get it.

My soul to God;
My soul to my Master and Mary.

Mary, mother of God,
May Jesus be with me
And me with Jesus.
(From the Irish.)

Mary, Brigid and Joseph support me in the presence of the glorious God. Sitting or lying, by night or by day, let me dwell with all and always.
(From the Irish).

O Mary, glorious, mild and beautiful,
My sustenance, my treasure,
My star of knowledge before me in this life,
In this valley of tears may you be my friend.
(From the Irish. IFC Ms, Vol. 72, p.304.)

Mary of Grace
Mother of the Son of God
May you take me in your care this day.

Son of the world, may your Father bless and save me always.

O Brigid, Mary of the Gael, wrap me in your cloak.

> I rise with Christ
> May Christ rise with me;
> The hand of God around me
> Asleep or awake.

May God's bounty and St Patrick's blessing be with me.

May I always do God's business.

May I be taught from the book of God.

Mary of the sweet Son, protect me from all sides.

May you counsel us, Lord God and be mindful of us.

The blessings of Peter and Paul, Mary and Son on us all.

That I may have the richness of health and know it.

If my neighbour has knowledge, let me not be too proud to light my candle from it.

God give me health, wealth and happiness but make sure they don't make me sick, poor and miserable.

> Seven blessings told seven times over,
> Mary left to her Son of old,
> Brigid to the length of her cloak.
> God to His own great might

Between us and the little people,
Us and the people of the wind,
Us and the evil hour of temptation,
Us and the drowning power of water,
Us and the earth's withering breath,
Us and the slave's cruel death.

(Said before undertaking a journey.)

May I never take life too seriously, knowing I'll never get out
of it alive.

May God be good to us.

Oh King of Sunday come to me with your help
And ease each gnawing pain.
Bright King of Monday always be true,
From your protection may I never stray.
Oh King of Tuesday with loving heart
Shelter me on the Day of Judgement.
Oh King of Wednesday let me not dwell
In slavery far from my people.
Oh King of Thursday I beg forgiveness,
Your honest laws I have broken by sin.
Oh King of Friday, keep not the tally
Of each deliberate act, each silly folly.
Oh King of Saturday, always I pray of you
To steer me safely beyond Acheron's shore;
May your sacrifice guard and protect me
In Paradise, for eternity.

(From the Irish of Tomás Rúa Ó Súilleabháin.)

I call on the seven daughters of the ocean
Who knit the stitches of the sons of longevity.
May three deaths be taken from me,
Three lifetimes given to me,
Seven waves of good fortune bestowed on me!

May spectres not harm me during my journey
Without hindrance, in Laserian's breastplate
May my name not be promised in vain!
May old age be mine
And death not come to me until I reach it.

I call on immortal Argetnia
To grant me time
As fine as white bronze!
May my form be planned
May my right be praised,
May my strength be augmented
May my tomb not be prepared
May I not die on my journey,
May my return be granted!
May the headless serpent not catch me,
Nor the green water-beetle
Nor the foolish cockroach!
May no robber harm me,
Nor troop of women,
Nor troop of warriors!
May the King of everything
Cast more time my way.

(From the Irish.)

May Brigit save us beyond troops of demons; may she break
before us the battles of every death.

    May she do away with the rent sin has put on us; the
blossomed branch; the Mother of Jesus; the dear young
woman greatly looked up to. That I may be safe in every
place with my saint of Leinster.
(Lady Gregory.)

The grace of God and Christ be on my soul.

Oh Father Eternity, save us.
(From the Irish.)

May we always have the love of God and of the neighbours.

May God leave us healthy until a year from today.

God give life and health to us all.

God bless my soul!
(Uttered in surprise.)

May God and His holy Mother save us at the hour of death.

The blessing of God and Mary on us.

Go bhfóire Dia orainn.
(God help us. Often said in dismay at some happening.)

God between us and all harm (or) God between us and the evil spirit.

May God save us from the evil intentions of others.

God's help on me.

Eternal Father, let your protective shield guard us night and day.

Son of God, attend to us.

Faoi bhrat Bhríde sinn!
(May we be under Brigid's cloak.)

May we receive the light of heaven (or) May God not quench the light of heaven on us.

May God strike me dumb if I tell a word of a lie.

> ... when I'm gone, oh! may some tongue,
> The minstrel's wish fulfil
> And still remember him who sang
> 'The Moon behind the Hill'.
> *(William Kenneally, 'The Moon behind the Hill.' Ballad.)*

> O Lord my God, in my loneliness,
> And darkling woe, I turn to Thee
> 'Tis Thou alone hast power to bless
> A heart oppressed with misery ...
> *(John K. Casey ['Leo'], 'A Poet's Prayer'.)*

> Get for me, O Mother Mary,
> A son before I go from this world.
> Do not delay to put his seed in my blood,
> O Womb in which the humanity of God was formed.
> *(Gill Bríghde Ó hEoghusa, 'A Prayer'.)*

> O God, give me the well of tears,
> To hide my sins;
> Abandon me not, like arid soil,
> Without soul or grace.
> *(Translated and adapted from James Carney.)*

May I live till I'm old and serve the God who rules heaven and may a welcome await me in eternal Paradise.
(Ibid.)

May one noble God and Father of nine ranks of holy spirits

protect me from fear, from caves of white death guard me
and keep me company.
(Ibid.)

    Please God, let me finish my days, I implore,
    In a place brings me joy
    In my own Ballymore.
(Padraic O'Farrell, 'Ballymore'.)

Blessings from the Poets

My blessing go with you, letter
To the lovely isle of Ealga
Woe not to see her peaks
And many red hills ...

Health to her gentry and people
Special health to her clerics.
Health to her refined womenfolk
Health to her learned men of poetry.
(From the Irish. Seathrun Ceitinn, 'Mo Bheannacht leat, a Scríbhinn'.)

Oh God and Christ with his binding sacrifice
Who truly saved both poor and naked,
Bring with you to sacred Paradise
Each creature of them who drowned.
(From the Irish. Antoine Ó Reachtabhra, 'Anach Cúain'.)

Angel of God protect us
And save us again till sunset
In the care of God and Mary
And Colmcille
Again till sunset.
(From the Irish. Anon.)

Your blessing, God, between ass and cow;
Your blessing, God to your child, mild prince;
Your blessing, God from Heaven to the house of pain;
Your blessing to the Holy Trinity.
(From the Irish. Anon. Christmas blessing.)

Bless this house, O Lord we pray
Make it safe by night and day.
Bless these walls so firm and stout,
Keeping want and trouble out.
Bless the roof and chimneys tall
Let Thy peace lie over all
Bless the doors that they may prove
Ever open to joy and love.
Bless the windows, shining bright
Letting in God's heavenly light
Bless the hearth a blazing there
With smoke ascending like a prayer.
Bless the people here within,
Keep them pure and free from sin;
Bless us all that we may be
Fit O Lord, to dwell with Thee.
Bless us all that we, one day,
May dwell, O Lord with thee.
(Anon. Sung by John McCormack.)

Céad Míle Faílte romhat,
Faílte is fiche romhat,
Naoí gcéad míle fáilte romhat,
Eileen Aroon.

(A hundred thousand welcomes to you/ Twenty-one welcomes to
you/ Nine hundred thousand welcomes to you, sweet Eileen.)

We may have great men, but we'll never have better,
Glory O! Glory O! To the Bold Fenian Men.
(Peadar Kearney.)

The blessings of a poor old man be with you night and day,
The blessings of a lonely man whose heart will soon be clay;
'Tis all the Heav'n I'd beg of God upon my dying day –
My soul to soar for evermore above you, Galway Bay.
(Francis Fahy, 'Galway Bay'.)

God bless my home in dear Cork city,
God bless the cause for which I die.
(Seamus Kavanagh, 'The Dying Rebel'.)

Now God be praised for your stout heart, brave little wife of
mine.
(Charles Kickham, 'Rory of the Hill'.)

Kidney of Bloom, pray for us.
Flower of the Bath, pray for us.
Mentor of Menton, pray for us.
Canvasser for the Freeman, pray for us.
Charitable Mason, pray for us.
Wandering Soap, pray for us.
Sweets of Sin, pray for us.
Music without Words, pray for us.
Reprover of the Citizen, pray for us.
Friend of the Fillies, pray for us.
Midwife most merciful, pray for us.
Potato Preservative against Plague and Pestilence, pray
for us.
(James Joyce, Ulysses.*)*

Ye pow'rs who over love preside,
Since mortal beauties drop so soon,
If you would have us well supplied,
Send us new nymphs with each new moon.
(Jonathan Swift, 'The Progress of Beauty'.)

' ... I'm thinkin' the love has gone to your head
When you dance a jig on the bones of the dead.'
Said I, 'By the Christ that is divine,
If I have a son, may he dance on mine.'
(Brendan Kennelly, Moloney Up and at It.*)*

In the name of the Father of victory,

In the name of the Son who got pain,
In the name of the Holy Spirit with strength,
Mary and her Son be with us during our trial.
(Translated from Dorcha Ó Meallain.)

Christ, Christ hear me!
Christ, Christ of Thy meekness!
Christ, Christ love me!
Sever me not from my sweetness.
(Anon. 'The Sweetness of Nature', Trans. Frank O'Connor.)

God of mercy! God of peace!
Make this mad confusion cease;
O'er the mental chaos move,
Through it *speak* the light of love.
(William Drennan, 'The Wake of William Orr'.)

May the mighty God of Freedom
Speed them well
Never taking
Further vengeance on his people of Tirawley.
(Samuel Ferguson, 'The Vengeance of the Welshmen of Tirawley'.)

A blessing on you, woman – do not speak!
*(Daniel Ó Liathaite, Abbot of Lismore, Ninth Century, 'Beannacht Fort'.
From the Irish.)*

O King that was born
To set bondsmen free,
In the coming battle,
Help the Gael!
(P. H. Pearse, 'Christmas 1915'.)

... Earth lie lightly on that breast,
And, kind Heaven, grant that spirit rest!
(Emily Jane Brontë, *'Shall Earth no more Inspire Thee'*.)

Then let my winds caress thee;
Thy comrade let me be –
Since nought beside can bless thee,
Return and dwell with me.
(Ibid.)

Sacred Heart of the Crucified Jesus, take away our hearts o'
stone ... an' give us hearts o' flesh! ... take away this
murdherin hate ... an' give us Thine own eternal love!
(Seán O'Casey, Juno and the Paycock, Act 2.)

O sages standing in God's holy fire
As in the gold mosaic of a wall,
Come from the holy fire, perne in a gyre,
And be the singing masters of my soul.
(W. B. Yeats 'Sailing to Byzantium'.)

Rancour, violence, death and sin
Are commonplace today.
Lord, help my parents change the world
And take these things away.
(Padraic O'Farrell, 'Puzzled Child's Prayer'.)

God bless now Desmond

– and you Sam our navigator our valiant necessary
wanderer to the edges of this interpreted world

God bless
(Desmond Egan, 'Echo's Bones'.)

Blest for ever is she who relied
Upon Erin's honour and Erin's pride.
(Thomas Moore, 'Rich and Rare'.)

People, Places and Politics

Help, friends and the love of God and the Farrells with you.

May Fr Eternity give you your share of eternity.
(From the Irish, Glen Colmcille area.)

> Blessings of Granny Doherty,
> She was the stuff;
> She hunted the Orangemen
> Over the bluff.

Angels of heaven bless the bare flags of Aran.

Athenry that was, Galway that is and Aran that will be, God bless us all.

May the Lord in His mercy be kind to Belfast.
(Maurice Craig, 'Ballad to a Traditional Refrain'.)

May the shadow of John Redmond never fall on your sons.
(May they never be recruited for the British army.)

May every Mayoman's pile be as high as Croagh Patrick and may his sorrows be as scarce as elephants in Murrisk.

Bless the men from Ballinglen, put whiskey in my tay.

> 'Long may you live, Leinster's hero,'
> Is a nation's prayer for thee;
> You are Ireland's pride and glory,
> Seán MacEoin of Ballinalee.
> *(Richard McGough, fellow-prisoner of MacEoin's.)*

Bless the men from Kerry,
And bless the men from Clare,
Those on the Aran islands,
The fine men from Kildare.
Bless the lads from Wicklow,
From Donegal as well;
From the whole damned part of Ireland
And the rest can go to hell.

No king could be more blessed than we,
Me and my charming Belfast Lass.
('The Charming Belfast Lass', c. 1825.)

Then here's to old Ireland, the land we love best
And dear Northern Athens, the pride of the west;
Prosperity beams on her, long may it last –
Success to the Town and the Trade of Belfast.
(T.C. Corry.)

Please God I'll soon return unto
The homes of Donegal.
(Seán MacBride, 'The Homes of Donegal'.)

May God bless the cause of freedom for which I am
sentenced to death.
(Anon. 'Lay Him Away o'er the Hillside'.)

Take my blessing with you, my beautiful boy, my blessing
and my benediction; the half of it for Ireland seven times
over; the other half once for Scotland ...
(Colmcille's blessing. Lady Gregory.)

Oh Donnybrook, jewel, full of mirth is your quiver,
Where all flock from Dublin to gape and to stare
At two elegant bridges, without e'er a river:
So success to the humours of Donnybrook Fair ...
Oh Donnybrook capers to sweet catgut-scrapers,

They bother the vapours and drive away care;
And what is more glorious – there's naught more uproarious –
Huzza for the humours of Donnybrook Fair!
(Anon. Nineteenth Century.)

God bless the grey mountains of dark Donegal
God bless royal Aileach, the pride of them all;
(Charles Gavan Duffy, 'Innishowen'.)

Here's a health to you, Father O'Flynn
Sláinte and sláinte and sláinte again.
(A P Graves.)

Ireland, long a province, be a nation once again.
(Thomas Davis.)

May the stones of Tory never point at you.
(It was believed that the 'Cursing Stones' of Tory brought bad luck if pointed at an enemy.)

Brigit, excellent woman; sudden flame; may the bright fiery sun bring us to the lasting kingdom.

May you have a Keogh for a neighbour.
(Blood from a Keogh was alleged to have healing properties.)

'God bless it' left unsaid, so Meelick tower was left unfinished.

Up the rebels, to Hell with the Pope,
And God Save – as you prefer – the King or Ireland.
(Louis MacNeice, 'Autumn Journal XVI'.)

More Blessings for Special Occasions

Most of the following are loosely translated from Béaloideas Iml. XIV *pp. 130-155 where they appeared in Irish. Some were used only in the Teelin, Co. Donegal area but others were used widely.*

Good luck be on your hand and may you not die in sin and may you never sprain your hand that shared with the poor.
(Said by a person who receives alms.)

May God save yourself and your crew from drowning.
(Said to fishermen going to sea.)

May God give you luck and may the fish of the great sea face you (or) May God and Mary protect you.
(Said to fishermen.)

May God and His holy women protect you until you return (or) May God bring you safely home and give you every sort of luck.
(Uttered to fishermen going to sea.)

The peace of God with my soul! (or) God bless you!
(Said in astonishment on hearing of some marvel.)

May God save you from harm.
(Said when a favour is done.)

May God and His Holy Mother save us from the power of fire and water.
(Uttered on hearing thunder.)

Rath Dé ort!
(The grace of God on you. *Said in thanks.*)

God grant that you do what is best.
(Said to a person who has a serious decision to make.)

The Son of God be with us.
(Said in amazement at some news heard.)

May God protect us.
(Uttered on hearing of some calamity that befell others.)

May God look after us (or) May God see us.
(Said by members of a deprived household.)

A thousand blessings with the name of Paul.
(Said when speaking about a person with epilepsy, which was called Paul's disease.)

As ucht Dé bailigh leat!
(For God's sake, leave me alone. *Said when told of a minor mishap.*)

May God leave them to you.
(Said on meeting a parent accompanied by children.)

God's blessing on you.
(Said to a person with a sore on a limb.)

May God never limit you.
(Uttered as encouragement to someone who has failed in any way.)

May God never answer you (or) May God never heed you (or) May God or Mary punish you.
(Uttered to a person who has said something offensive.)

Do not come between the hope of God.
(Said when bad weather threatens the saving of crops or turf or the catching of fish.)

God is strong and has a good Mother (or) God is good.
(Said in hope by someone who has suffered a material loss.)

May God place a hand on him.
(Said about a person who is so sick that he would be better off dead.)

The Cross of the Crucifixion of Christ be on you.
(Uttered by a mother while making the sign of the Cross on a child not yet able to do so himself.)

May God deliver him (from an illness).

May God settle him.
(Said of a person in trouble.)

God give you the price (or) May it be the price of you.
(Said to a person who has accomplished something worthwhile.)

May God increase your store and save those who are minding you.
(Said to somebody who has received an unexpected windfall.)

May God and Mary save us and all belonging to us from the evil of the night.
(Said at the end of the recitation of the Rosary.)

God's gift to you.
(Said to a musician or other talented person who has entertained.)

God be praised (or) Praise be to God.
(Uttered on hearing of something marvellous.)

May you receive the weight of your alms of God's grace.
(Said in thanks by a person who receives alms.)

May God put fruit and blossom on the seed we are about to sow.
(Uttered as potato sets are taken down for sowing.)

May God leave health to all we see (or) May God leave health to your stock.
(Uttered when meeting someone driving stock.)

May your abode please you.
(Said to somebody who moves house.)

May your journey rise with you and may God give you luck.
(Said to somebody about to emigrate.)

Bloom and blessing, night and day, on you.
(Said, especially to children, when a good turn is done.)

Place your will with the will of God.
(Said on hearing about the death of somebody.)

May God never let us see the likes again.
(Said on hearing or seeing something frightening.)

May God save you without the devil (or) May God make it easy on you.
(Said to people in trouble.)

May your soul find eternal glory.
(Said in thanks for help.)

The shape of Christ be on his coat.
(Uttered when somebody good or holy is mentioned or seen.)

The grace of God and Mary on the work.
(Uttered when about to undertake some work.)

Father of truth, deliver us from all evil.
(Uttered when bad news is heard.)

May God forgive me (for doing this wrong).
(Said when something is said that might cause scandal.)

> *Dia liom!* (God be with me)
> *Dia liom!*
> *Dia agus Muire liom!* (God and Mary be with me!)
(Uttered as each of three pinches of snuff are snorted.)

May God give us enough body and soul to bear our cross
patiently.
(Said when a bereavement or other catastrophe occurs in a family.)

The fruit of your hand, O God, on this year's crops.
(Said when digging the first of the new potatoes.)

That God may strike me dead.
(Swearing truth.)

> God and Mary bless you, motherless child,
> Your cry is not so sweet, nor is your laughter bright.
(Aindrias Ó Muimhneacháin.)

My foot on land,
My foot on sea,
God and Mary cure the blackleg
And the root of your calf's tongue.
(Vol., III. Béaloideas, 1931-32.)

May all your bad luck go with him.
(Said to a neighbour on burying a beast of his.)

The King of the World, King of Brightness, King of Heaven
and Paradise, King of Saints born in the stable bless all here.
(Said on entering a house on Christmas Eve. Answer:)

May the same King bless you.

Be you cheerful!
(Said on entering a house. Answer:)

The King's cheer to you!
(IFC Ms, Vol. 991, p. 223.)

May your man not forsake the home on Christmas night.
(It was considered unlucky to do so.)

May not more numerous be
The grains of sand by the sea,
Or the blades of grass on the lea,
Or the drops of dew on the tree,
Than the blessings upon the soul
And the souls of the dead with thee,
And my soul when life shall flee.
(Said after smoking. Douglas Hyde.)

Amusing Blessings

If I bless you with a song
That's not short and not too long
It's 'cause quite often I wander a bit off key.
If the air causes alarm,
It will not do you much harm
'Cause the penance might save you from Purgatory.

Many happy returns of the day and may it miss you when it comes.

If you marry, may you marry last year.

That you may never see a bad day and if it sees you may it be wearing glasses.

Good luck to you, your blood is worth bottling and may glass splinters blind hell's stokers.

Bless De Valera and Seán MacEntee
Bless their brown bread and their half ounce of tea.
(From a wartime parody commenting on food rationing.)

May the wind be always at your back, especially coming home on Saturday night.

A thousand blessings, maybe more,
Come down on you, *mo grádh, mo stór*;
Especially if you give your hand
To tend me and my plot of land.

Ireland is rearing them yet and when she's done may you wed the best of them.

May you live to be a hundred years and one extra year to atone.

> Saints of glory protect us,
> Holy Angels from the throne of God, guide us,
> And if the devil still gets within a stone's throw of us
> May there be nothing but sand to peg (throw) at us.

May St Peter never ask you to light a fire on a lake or advise a headstrong woman.

May you always keep out from the priests; that way you will keep in with them.

May you never stay seeing the bees without spotting the honey.

May you dance with all the saints in heaven bar St Vitus.

> Bless the man who ploughs the furrow;
> Ferrets rabbits from a burrow.
> Bless his wife, may she not often
> Ferret his last penny off him.

That you may have the appetite of a horse; that's better than having too much to eat!

May you be as well as you can bear to be.

May the hand that offers trouble be as idle as the left hand of a bodhran.

May the lips that speak ill of you never say thanks to St Peter.

May your horse always stand in the middle of the fair.

May you find a good sonuachar (spouse) – what my mother-in-law's son got.
(A woman who says this, praises herself.)

Let your enemies hear the bees but may you get the honey.

That your patch of trouble may not cover the hole in a leprechaun's breeches.

May you get what you're after with the help of God and two policemen.

> Bless the horse that farts at noon,
> Twice bless the one that farts at eve,
> And thrice bless the work that makes him fart.

Toasts and Hearty Wishes

Whiskey, you're the divil,
You're leading me astray;
Over hills and mountains,
And to Americay.
You're sweeter, stronger, dacenter;
You're spunkier nor tay.
Oh whiskey, you're me darlin' drunk or sober!

In a chapter called 'Sláinte' from his book Irish Life and Lore *(Cork 1982), Séamas Ó Catháin imparts valuable information on the origin and use of Irish toasts. These are not of the stuffy nature observed at formal dinners, but are genuine expressions of good fellowship and heartiness. Séamas quotes a conversation recorded in IFC Ms. Vol. 800, between folklorists Niall Ó Dubhthaigh and Seán Ó hEochaidh:*

In my young days, when two or three men went in for a drink together, it was the custom for them to go into a back room – a snug. They never stood at the counter. Each of them would strike three hefty blows on the table and, in a flash, the barmaid would be in to see what they wanted. She would be ordered to bring them a half-pint of whiskey and, in due course, she would return with a jug and a glass. Should there be ten men in the company, they would still only have the one glass. The man who had ordered and paid for the drink would then stand up and hand a glass of whiskey to the man nearest to him, who would then say – 'Here's health' (Seo do shláinte) to which the first man might answer, 'God grant you health' (Sláinte ó Dhia duit) ...

Long ago, when poteen was plentiful and whiskey was cheap, there would be drink at every *meitheal* (gathering of neighbours for work). The men didn't get paid, but at least they got a good drink. They used to drink toasts on such occasions too and the man might raise his glass like this – 'Good health boys, one and all, and may God bless you and the work.' (Bhur sláinte uilig go léir, a bhuachaillí, agus go gcuirí Dia rath oraibh féin agus ar bhur gcuid oibre) ...

At funerals, glasses were raised to the toast 'Eternal rest to the soul that has joined the host of the dead'. Match-making involved liberal imbibing and the toast 'Here's your health, may God give you luck and a safe journey and may God save the man that's going to settle down, from heart-break, harm and need'.

The first seven toasts below are from the *Irish Folklore Collection* as quoted in Séamas Ó Catháin's book.

Here's to the pigeon of the green wing,
A Roman priest and a Fenian king,
Here's to King William –
With a knife in his heart and a fork in his liver,
That he may never die or no one kill him,
Till he goes to hell and the devil gets 'melling' him.

Here's from the roof rib to the foundation stone,
All sorts of bother and misfortune,
Hell's blazes and damnation to any man who has a
    daughter –
And won't give her to me.

Here's health and prosperity ,
To you and all your posterity,
And them that doesn't drink with sincerity
That they may be damned for all eternity.

Long, long ago, in Queen Anne's time,
When a Catholic might lose his head,
Dan, in his prime, said, 'That's a crime –
For when taking a tot, let Sasanach or Scot,
Drink a toast or else,' said he,
'On the crown of their head,
With their arse in the air,
It's in hell that they shall be.'

Here's to you as good as you are,
And to me as bad as I am;
I'm as good as you are,
Bad and all as I am.

The health of bright glory to you.

Here's to the High Son who stretched his limbs for crucifixion on the cross, And here's the health of the Virgin Mother, And here's the health of St Patrick who blessed Ireland.

Whisky, drink divine!
Why should drivellers bore us
With the praise of wine
When we've thee before us.
(Joseph O'Leary ,'Whisky, Drink Divine'.)

Praise God, all true Protestants
And I will toast no further
For, had the Papists won the day;
There'd have been bloody murder.
(Toast based on the nineteenth century ballad 'The Boyne Water'.)

Good health to your enemies' enemies.

Hold your hour and have another!

Cheers and tobacco spits!

Wet your whistle well and may we never die of the drought!

Mo grá thú!
(My love to you!)

The health of the salmon and the trout
That swim to and fro' near the Bull's Mouth;*
Do not ask for a pot, mug or jug,
Down the hatch – drink up!

(* *In Achill.*)

Sláinte!
([Your] health!)

Have another drink and may St Peter think it's tay (tea)!

Drink, as in bumpers past troubles we drown,
A health to the lads that made croppies lie down.

(*Anon. 'Croppies lie Down', an Orange ballad.*)

Here's your health for consideration!

Health to you and yours; to mine and ours.
If mine and ours ever come across you and yours,
I hope that you and yours will do as much for mine and ours
As mine and ours have done for you and yours.

(*Not recommended for late-night toasts!*)

Here's to the next one and may you be granted a trooper's pardon!

Drink up! It's always the next one that sickens you.

Whiskey is the life of man,
Whiskey Johnny!
Whiskey in an old tin can,
Whiskey for my Johnny.

(*Belfast docks toast.*)

Health and long life to you
Land without rent to you
A child every year to you
And may you die in Ireland.

Good luck whatever!

Good health without a cold in your pipes!

Your good health from person to person and if any person
doesn't wish it, let him speak up!

Here's to the first drop – the one that destroys you; there's
no harm at all in the last!

May they be drinking bog-water, while you're supping the
uisce beatha (whiskey).

Here's one for the road and may you know every turning!

I'll drink and I'll drink and I'll drink to your health, love
And were you on board ship, I'd drink to you the better!
(Sailors' toast. From the Irish.)

Here's mud in one eye and a glint in the other!

Here's to the maiden of bashful fifteen;
Here's to the widow of fifty;
Here's to the flaunting, extravagant quean,
And here's to the housewife that's thrifty.
Let the toast pass – drink to the lass,
I'll warrant she'll prove an excuse for the glass.
(Richard Brinsley Sheridan, The School for Scandal, *Act 3, Scene 3.)*

Here's to the hand that made the ball,
That shot Lord Leitrim in Donegal.
(A Donegal toast.)

Then come, put the jorum about,
And let us be merry and clever
Our hearts and our liquors are stout
Here's the Three Jolly Pigeons forever.
(Oliver Goldsmith, She Stoops to Conquer, *Act 1, Scene 1.)*

May we forget the bitterness of paying for it!

May the roof above us never fall in
And may us good companions beneath it
Never fall out.

Thirst begets thirst
So be getting yours first;
Good luck! Stay sane!
Down the dusty lane!

May the next drop make the grass grow long on the road to
hell for you!

Here's the health of Ireland except County Mayo,
And whoever doesn't like that may he not be long alive.
(From the Irish, often replied to by Mayo drinkers as follows:)

Ireland's health and County Mayo,
And when that is lost, may we be alive;
The health of the hag from County Meath
And not out of love for her but her drop,
Your health from wall to wall
And the one outside the closed door, speak!

The glorious, pious and immortal memory of the great and good King William! – not forgetting Oliver Cromwell, who assisted in redeeming us from popery, slavery, arbitrary power, brass money and wooden shoes! May we never want a Williamite to kick the **** of a Jacobite! – and a **** for the *Bishop of Cork*! And he that won't drink this, whether he be priest, bishop, deacon, bellows-blower, grave digger or any other of the fraternity of *the clergy*; may a north wind blow him to the south and a west wind blow him to the east! May he have a dark night – a lee shore – a rank storm and a leaky vessel, to transport him over the river Styx! May the dog Cerebus make a meal of his r--p , and Pluto a snuff-box of his skull! and may the devil jump down his throat with a red-hot harrow, with every pin to tear out a gut, and blow him with a *clean* carcass to hell! *Amen*!

(Jonah Barrington's Orange Toast, to 'The glorious, pious, and immortal memory of William the Dutchman'. Described as 'making sentiments' this toast was countered by:)

The memory of the chestnut horse that broke the neck of the same King William!

>We'll toast Old Ireland!
>Dear Old Ireland!
>Ireland boys, Hurrah!

(T.D. Sullivan 'Song from the Backwoods'.)

Here's to the same again or something similar!

Sláinte an bhradáin agat – croí folláin agus gob fliuch.
(The health of the salmon to you – a sound heart and a wet mouth!)

Good luck to you and bad shoes to your advisers.
(Said to a drinking companion who complains about drink being bad for a man.)

Here's health and the drunk's curse on Killarney to the begrudgers!

>The health of all Ireland and County Mayo
>When they are all dead, be us still on the go;
>From Royal County Meath
>The health of the hag;
>Not herself, but her drink
>Gives us reason to brag.
>So here's health, one and all,
>From one wall to another,
>And if you're outside the door,
>Shout loud, brother!
>Here's to youth! Let's drink to it
>With bumpers full brimming.

(From the Irish.)

Sláinte! And when the world's troubles are displayed on the floor, may you select your own.

Health! May your well never run dry!

>Colmcille sent you his blessing
>And instructed you to drink
>And the man who hasn't the price of it
>The other man will give it to him.

or

>The man whose pocket and purse are empty
>He cannot pay like the other men,
>Let this man here pay for that man there
>And God will pay for the last man then.

(Translated from Douglas Hyde.)

When, from heaven God looks down
On your very last half-crown,
By a miracle, may it suddenly clink
'Gainst another one and ten,
Against twenty, twice again –
Just as long as you keep paying for the drink!

Your property stay with you; may you rear children on it and may they be around to look after you. Drink up now to ensure as much!

I drink the health of often-who-came,
Who often-comes-not I also must name;
'Though often-comes-not I must also blame
For he comes not as often as often-who-came.

Peace on your hand!

Saint Patrick was a gentleman;
Through strategy and strength
He drove the snakes from Erin
A toast, then, to his health.
But not too many toasts, now
Or you'll lose your sense and then
Forget about Saint Patrick
And meet all those snakes again.

May God never knock you down as long as you keep putting them up!

Proposal: To healthy stock and may they never need saving!
Reply: During drinking hours!

I'll give you your health and may your enemies be beggars!

The face of the sad story be turned away from us!

Proposal: May you flourish like the fern!
Reply: God let you profit!

Your life and your health to you!

When you drop down from it (the drink) may there be the seventh son of a seventh son beside you ere the glass hits the floor.

> The health of all salmon,
> The health of all trout
> That swim back and forth
> Near the wide river mouth.
> Ask not for a saucepan,
> A jug or a cup;
> Down the hatch, my fine hero
> Drink! Drink it all up!

May there never be a welt on the hand that pays for the drinks.

> Health to the man who buys his round
> To heaven's alehouse be he bound.

Here's your health from the heel to the back of the knee, and may we not leave this place until we are drunk.
(From the Irish. Béaloideas *IML. XIV p.142.)*

If you're on your ear before you leave, may it be hearing sweet words of comfort.

May you live as long as you want
And never want as long as you live.

So, all true blues, come fill your glass,
A better toast will never pass;
We'll drink unto the lovely lass,
The Orange Maid of Sligo.
(From 'The Orange Maid of Sligo'. Nineteenth century ballad.)

May we always have a clean shirt, a clear conscience and a few bob in our pockets.
(Answered by:)

Or if not, a decent man to stand us a drink!

Drink as if it was your last one but may the last one not come till morning.

May you be poor in misfortune,
Slow to make enemies
Fast to make friends
But rich or poor, slow or fast
May you know nothing but happiness.

Seo sláinte mhinic-a-thig,
Agus seo sláinte minic-nach-dtig.
Is trua nach dtig minic-nach-dtig,
Leath chomh minic le minic-a-thig
(Health to often-comes,
And health to seldom-comes.
A pity that seldom-comes
Does not come half as often as often-comes.)

Drink up! May we die happy by living to see our own funerals.
(Possibly the only Irish bull in toast form!)

May God hold you in the hollow of His hand and have a drink in the other for you.

> Here's a health to youze who waves the Union Jack
> If youze pays for us who wears the Green;
> Buy another round and here's your health again
> And we'll all sing *God Save the Queen!*
>
> O long life to the man who invented poteen
> Sure the Pope ought to make him a martyr;
> If I myself was this moment Victoria, our Queen,
> I'd drink nothing but whiskey and water.
>
> *(Michael Moran [Zozimus], 'In Praise of Poteen'.)*

> I give you the disproportion between labour spent
> And joy at random ...
>
> *(Louis MacNeice, 'Train to Dublin'.)*

> They talk of the Romans of ould,
> Whom, they say, in their own times was frisky,
> But trust me to keep out of the cowld,
> The Romans at home here like whiskey...
> Oh! poitin, good luck to ye, dear!
>
> *(Charles Lever, 'Poitin, Good Luck to ye, Dear!')*

> A true man like you, man
> Will lift your glass with us!
>
> *(John Kells Ingram, 'The Memory of the Dead'.)*

> To every one a full measure!
> Not drinking? Then what is your pleasure?
> You're short did you say?
> Can't afford it today?
> What harm, you can pay at your leisure.
>
> *(From the Irish. Translated by James N. Healy, Ballads from the Pubs of Ireland.)*

At the end of the day,
Let us drink to work well done,
And if you are an idler,
We'll toast tomorrow's fun.

Good luck to us all and bad luck to nobody.

We have our health, we have our memories, we have our
wives to bring us home.
(Seán Nicholson, August 1992.)

General Curses

Animals, Birds etc.

A fox on your fishing hook.
(Claddagh fisherman's curse. Patrick C Power.)

May all the goats in Gorey chase you to hell.

May you buy every hair in your cow's tail.
(Pay dearly for stock.)

May your hens get the disorder, your cows the crippen (phosphorosis) and your calves the white scour and may you yourself go blind so that you'll not know your woman from a haystack.
(Edited from IFC Ms. Vol. 1403.)

May you ride Rogan's gander to the dickens.

May you find the bees but miss the honey.

> For stealing the wether, you lying scraper,
> Down in hell I will you for your agony;
> In the bottom of the cauldron with Oscar* blowing (the
>   flames),
> And twenty-one mad demons picking at you.

(Son of Oisin, a warrior of the Fianna.)*

That you may ever be a mile from a cow's track – and the Lord doesn't cross fields.

Curse of the crows (or ravens) on you.

The plight of the boiled and broken minnow to you.

May you hang a dog and drown a bitch.

A magpie on your wheatfield gate.

Black cows to you.

> Oh Mary Dunlea, may harm overtake you
> A child crossways in you and never born;
> Or if so, may he not be like a Christian.
> The snout of a pig and the mouth of a sheep on him,
> The snout of a pig rooting in the dung.
> For fear he would be a hangman that would hang the
> people!

May the man who would curse the bladder out of a goat have a chat with you before Christmas.

May the back of you get a salmon's roasting.

May the ass that pulls your coffin-cart have no cross on its back.

If ever you're on the pig's back, I hope it's heading for the curing-house.

Garlacon (a lingering disease) to your stock.

May your horse have a sagging nosebag.

That your cat may bury you with its clap.

A kitten's death to you.

May the cats eat the women.
(Power, p.85.)

The curse of the goose that lost the quill that wrote the ten commandments on you.

Upon my soul! By Gannies! By the holy farmer! By the hokey! Upon my cloak! By the gods of war! *Mo léir!*
(Alas!)

Death

That you may die roarin' like Doran's ass.

That your bread may be baked.
(That you may die.)

For many a day may you rest in the clay.

Bás na bpisín chugat.
(The kittens' death to you, i.e. May you drown. [*Power p.83*])

Six horse loads of burial clay on you.

May there be red ribbons at your funeral.
(Red ribbons were once worn at obsequies of a murder victim.)

May they sing Eileen Aroon at your wake.
(Considered an unlucky song.)

May there never be enough of your people in heaven to make a half-set.

You'll be travelling yet with your two feet before you.

> May the curse of the crows in sorrow prostrate you now!
> Scorn, disgrace, malediction by churches and bells!
> Your old frame dead and lifeless with never a stir!
> With none to wake your corpse; your limbs without a
>   shroud.

(Eoghan Ruadh Ó Súilleabháin, Power, p.68.)

May the company at your wake pray on cold flags.
(You will not get many prayers said for you.)

> May his hens lay clods and stones
> May the east wind blight his bones
> May warts and welts waylay him by the score.
> Now I swear upon this verse
> He'll be travelling soon by hearse
> And we'll never see Sean Dota any more.

(John B. Keane, Sive, Act 2, Scene 2.)

May you rot in the pauper's plot.

Hungry grass grow around your grave.
(By custom, nobody would walk on it, therefore no prayers would be said.)

May you never be buried in the pound section.

You mean thing! May you soon find out there's no pockets in a shroud.

May you not see the corncrake or the cuckoo.

Let it not be long till you die, despite the Son of God.
(Power.)

Cripples and crooks carry your coffin.

That you may be a load for four before the year is out.
(Four coffin-bearers.)

That you may fester in your grave.

The loss of the stream on him.
(That he may drown.)

Strangulation and drowning to you.

May you die without a priest in a town with no clergy.

May the foam of the river settle on you.
(May you drown.)

May there be a corpse here each Monday morning.
(Said to have been uttered to St Patrick by a Corkman. The saint replied: 'May it be a starling's'.)

May the only tears at your graveside be the onion-pullers'.

My grief, my brother,

My curse on death,
Seven cursed be the plague.
(Michael Kirby.)

Íde coileach Éamoinn ort.
(The fate of Ned's cock to you; a reference to a cock admiring his
reflection in water until he fell in and was drowned. *[Power]*)

A slippy handle on your *sleán*.
(If a sleán fell, it was believed that a family death would follow.)

May the snails devour his corpse,
And the rain do harm worse;
May the devil sweep the hairy crature soon;
He's as greedy as a sow;
As the crow behind the plough;
That black man from the mountain, Seánín Rua!
(John B. Keane, Sive, *Act 1, Scene 3.)*

Health and Wealth

May you have a little skillet,
May you have little in it.
May you have to break it,
To find the little bit in it.

The consumption on you.

May your spuds be like rosary-beads on the stalk.

If your crop is tall
Be your *meitheal* small.

May the only gold you ever win
Be that what sticks to the callow's whin.

At the going down of the sun may you have nothing in your
bag and less in your pocket.

That your pocket may drag your face into tripping you up.
(*i.e. that your wealth may bring you unhappiness.*)

May you some day follow the crow for your supper and get
bitten by a jackdaw.

The hand of God fall on you and your money.

May your trouble be in your throat.

May you never see the light of heaven till you pay me what
you owe me.

Stillborn or dawny (miserable, weak) stock to you.

May you live to see the two days.
(*Said to a wealthy person, wishing poverty.*)

Hell and the Devil

May the devil behead all landlords and make a day's work
of their necks.

May you dance with a devil on your back.

God damn you.

Blast you to hell.

The devil take you.

That the midil may tasp you, you glodach crois ould beoir.
(Tinkers' Cant: That the devil may take you, you dirty old woman.)

May the seven terriers of hell sit on the spool of your breast
and bark in at your soul-case.
(IFC Ms, Vol. 1403.)

May the devil throw you into the pit of ashes seven miles
below hell.
(John M. Feehan.)

May they all go to hell and not have a drop of porter to
quench their eternal thirst.

May the devil weave your shroud and may he pin the seams
together
(A double curse, since using pins in a shroud was considered unlucky.)

May you rot in hell for that, you miserable bastard.

That you may never see the inside of heaven.

Hell's bells to you.

I'll see you to hell.

The devil swallow you sideways.

You'll roast in hell for that, so you will.

You'll dance on the Old Boy's *leac na tine*.
(The slab in front of the hearth which covered the ash-pit and gave a resonance when danced upon, normally by the man of the house.)

To Halifax with you.
(Here the word 'hell' is disguised.)

God damn your soul to hell.

Your soul to the devil (or) The devil take your soul.

Come hell or high water, may you be ruined.

The Old Boy settle your hash for you and have your guts for garters.

The devil fool you.

The devil tear you.

When the bottom falls out of Purgatory, may you join the poor Papists in hell.

The devil mend you.

May your next settle (bed) be at the hob of hell.

Hell's hottest corner for you.

The devil set a place for you in hot contrary corner.

The devil's plague on you.

Your heart to the devil.

The devil come to you.

May the devil's coach-horse come at a canter to your wake.

Go to hell and be damned.

Paddy Ryan's supper to you – hard knocks and the devil to eat.

I'd ask Old Nick to make drisheens out of you only your blood is too watery.

> Well I hope that Old Nick,
> Pokes your eyes with his stick.
> Cuts your nose with a shears
> And burns off your big ears.

May the devil damn you to the stone of dirges, or to the well of ashes seven miles below hell; and may the devil break your bones! And all my calamity and harm and misfortune for a year on you.
(Power.)

> In hell may you be because of your sins!
> May the devil have your soul under guard there!
> For you treacherously swore that the head of the Crop-
>   pies
> Was Power whom you couldn't disparage.

(Concerning the betrayer of a 1798 patriot. Power.)

The devil shake you by the heels.

That you may roast in hell for that and have your gravy sucked by the devil.

The devil's flame on you.

The tide of the devil engulf you.

The devil's cagger (pedlar's haberdashery) on you.

The devil give you oats.
(Uttered to a horse.)

By the livin' divils!

May the keystone of heaven's arch fall on you and push you down below.

The devil take the hindmost.

I'll carry you to the devil and may he take you out of my sight.

May the devil break the hasp of your back.
(James Joyce.)

Home

May you never call a hearth your own.

May you never have more than point with your praties.
(*'Point' was just as much butter as would sit on the point of a knife.*)

May you long be homeless.

Ill-Luck

Ill-luck to your mother for bearing you.

May your first born belong to the *lios (na sídhe)*.
(*To the fairies.*)

May you go stone blind so that you won't know your wife
from a headstone.
(*John M. Feehan.*)

'Viction to you.
(*Eviction.*)

A heart-scald on you.

Harm and loss to you with lasting grief.

Scréach mhaidne chugat.
(The morning screech on you.)

May there be guinea-fowl crying at your child's birth.
(*A bad luck sign.*)

That he may end up on the gallows.

A high noose and gallows and a windy day outside (to you).

    A taut, swift, suitable gallows-rope
    Around the narrow, scrawny neck of the hanging
      scoundrel.

May you break your kneecap going down the steep steps of your rosiest garden.

May the bard's curse on the man who stole his harp fall on you.

Cold days and nights without a fire to you.

That you may meet your fetch at evening.
(Believed to bring bad luck.)

Monday's curse on you.

Bad cess to you.

Bad scran to you.

Increasing calamity to you.

Be you caught between Caravat and Shanavest and neither liking you.
(Two famous factions.)

May you wind up like Weakie Willy Walsh – the breath only just in and out of him and the grass not knowing he was walking over it.

May he screech with awful thirst
May his brains and eyeballs burst
That melted amadán, that big bostoon,
May the fleas consume his bed
And the mange eat up his head,
That blackman from the mountain, Seánín Rua.

(John B. Keane, Sive, Act 2, Scene 2.)

Marriage

May you marry a malfuastar.
(A flurrysome person.)

May you marry in haste and repent at leisure.

May you marry far from the ashpit.
(A stranger.)

May you marry a wench that blows wind like a stone from a sling.

Your eyes damp with tears
Your fingers trembling
Your body barren
Your breasts milkless
With never a son
Nor ever the strength
To please your man.

May the Black Hag of Beara curse this alliance.

May you marry a mountainy woman so that you'll marry the whole mountain.

Morning screams to you.

> May she marry a ghost and bear him a kitten and may
> The High King of glory permit her to get the mange.
>
> *(James Stephens, 'A Glass of Beer'.)*

May you marry a frigid widow-woman left a *bánóg* of thistles.

Pissmires and spiders be in your marriage-bed.

May you marry a Roman (and have to quit your place and disgrace your family).
(An Orange curse.)

May you have the runs on your wedding-night.
(Diarrhoea.)

In your house, may the grey mare be the better horse

or

May the long haired chum lead your gallop.
(May the woman be boss in your home.)

Miscellaneous

> A high windy gallows to you.
> By the sod you stand on, curse not
> You tread it but for a short while
> But lie beneath it for eternity.
>
> *(From the Irish. Retort to a curse uttered.)*

The madness of the brain on him,
A broken heart in him,
A heart-scourge beside him,
A hangman's noose around him.

O wretch of the crooked foot, the crippled knee and the squinting eye, a thousand curses on you, torn clothes on your back and a pox on every bit of you.

Curse of Cromwell on you.

Curse of God on you.

Curse of Christmas on you.
(Said when unwilling to utter the Holy Name.)

O cursed hag who prays not to Mary, may your teeth fall out and may you disappear across the sea.

Curse of Moll Anthony on you.
(County Kildare curse.)

Curse of Biddy Early on you.
(County Clare curse.)

Curse of Madge Moran on you.
(County Meath curse.)

May I bend a coin on the Holy Ghost for you.
(Said as a sixpenny piece is hidden in a church to curse someone.)

A heart-scald to you.

Curse of the seven snotty orphans on you.

Cold days and nights to you.

A red nail through the tongue that said it.

God's curse and His church's be on you.

Curse of the Seven Septs of the Laois Crosbies on you.

The seven curses of Quilty on you.

The curse of the O'Flahertys on you.
(The line of the powerful Galway clan was discontinued because of a priest's curse.)

Curse of the town on you.
(Uttered by a tinker who spent all his money carousing in a particular town.)

Curse of the wretched and the strong on the one who gave.

Curse of God on you.

God damn you.

Devil damn you.

Double damn on it.

May the curse of the woman on the one who seduced her man fall on you.

Bad luck to them that's cloddin' stones.
(Throwing stones – Belfast.)

May your trouble be in your throat.

Be the Lord boundin' jaysus!

Be the jumpin' jaysus.

Be the cross o' Christ!

Jesus wept (bitter tears)!

By the mockstick of war!

May God never give you his benefit.

Mallacht na Bantraí ort (The widow's curse on you).
(One form of the curse went as follows:)

> Spiteful Gerald of the jolly laugh,
> May the growth from your threshold to your gate
> Be bushes with two heads in the ground
> And a green lake to the top of your hall;
> Nest of a hawk in the chimney-hole,
> And a goat's lair at the head of your bed,
> Because you stole from me my son and his father
> You stole from me my twelve cows and the bull –
> So may no inheritance be left to your heir.

(From the Irish [anon].)

Abiding hatred fall on you.

Son of God make you blind.

Your mouth and your face under you.
(Be 'down in the mouth', therefore unhappy.)

He can quench the candle at the other side of the kitchen with a curse and I hope he comes to your *céilí*.

Back of my hand to you.

The priest's curse on you.

A host of curses on you.

Curse you and your future generations.

The curse of the White Woman on you.

Here's the dirty water to you (or) Poisoned destruction to you.
(A curse on the fairies, when throwing out water.)

The work of the trouble-makers on you.

Blindness (or some other malady) to you.

May the gates of paradise never open to you.

The wretched state of the sinner and the gallows knot to you.

God take the east and west from you –
The road before and behind you.

Three curses that cannot be countered:
The curse of a woman in labour.
The curse of a landless man.
The curse of a dead man.

Money and Poverty

The devil take your last shilling.

May you not have enough to buy your shroud.

May your Sunday best have its share of turtles.
(Threads hanging down – Antrim)

May your thatch leak,
And your boots squeak.
May your eyes forever squint
And may you never have the rint (rent).

That you may have forty-five ways of putting on your coat
this harvest-time.
(i.e. be in tatters.)

May all belonging to you have to live on the smell of an oily
rag.

That you may scratch a beggarman's back some day.
(i.e. be a beggar yourself.)

Faith, may you follow the crow for that some day.
(Uttered when seeing some food thrown away.)

Faith, may you get your come-uppance before your pride wears down.

People, Places and Politics

May the back of your shirt never pass Churchtown.
(Said by a priest to a parishioner who vowed to vote Tory.)

God damn the Whigs and Tories too.
(Jonathan Swift, 'Mad Mullinix and Timothy'.)

The curse of Swift is upon him – to have been born an Irishman; to have possessed a genius and to have used his talents for the good of his country.
(Henry Grattan writing of Dr Kirwan, 1792.)

The God of nature never intended that Ireland should be a province, and by God she never will.
(Thomas Goold at a meeting of the Irish Bar against the Act of Union, 9 December 1799.)

The Horserider's Reproach

O gelding, who has lost me my love
go to the devil, and leave my sight;
that you may ail a year hence
and by my father's soul, I play not.

Are you ashamed, stupid gelding,
O diabolical, coarse, reprobate
For leaving me turned over in the excrement
Right where my woman could see me?

Twenty death squeezes on you tonight
and forever in your rump my curse;

94

May ravens gouge out your two eyes,
You diabolical humpy harlot!

May there be a fiery nail ever in your hoof
and may the crupper cut your tail-muscle,
scores all over your back
and lightning in the mouth of your orifice!

That a grip of grass you may never get,
nor a grain of corn till Christmas,
nor a single drop of water for ever,
until you die of the dread drought.

That the spur of the right leg may hack
a cleft in your hip-joint;
A fireball in your backside –
Did you not see her in the window?
(Translated from Aodh Mac Gabhrain's 'Achasán an Mharcaigh'.)

A Kerryman swore robbery on a widow's son and got him
hanged. The widow cursed him and he got throat-cat (a
disease) and died of hunger.
(IFC Ms, Vol. 613, p. 210.)

That your fire may go out and that you may never again be
able to redden it within a mile of where you're standing.
*(St Lattern used to take coals from a smith to light her own fire. She
carried them in her apron. One morning she noticed the smith admiring
her ankles. The coals fell through her apron and she realised that she must
have committed the sin of pride so she cursed the smith. IFC Ms, Vol.
613, p. 311.)*

Oh! my curse on one black heart in Aghadoe, Aghadoe,
Oh Shaun Drum my mother's son, in Aghadoe,
When your throat fares in hell's drought, salt the flame
   be in your mouth,

For the treachery you did in Aghadoe!
(John Todhunter, 'Aghadoe'.)

If you take the king's shilling, may you spend it in hell.

Murrough, the poet, I pray God's colic on you.

Bad cess to that robber, old Cromwell, and to all his long battering train.
(Anon. 'Blarney Castle, My Darling'.)

'Tis with the devil you will fly away, you porter-swiping similitude of the bisection of a vortex!
(Anon. The Liberator and Biddy Moriarty.)

Carolan's curse on you.

The dog's bark on the O'Keefes to you.
(The O'Keefes were harsh landlords.)

May the curse of the *maighdean mhara* (mermaid. Lit: sea-virgin) on the O'Briens of Newhall plague you.
(In the guise of a wonderful cow, the mermaid provided the people of Clare, except the O'Briens, with milk during the Famine.)

The curse of the Mad Major on you.
(Major Denis O'Farrell, whose cursing of an adjutant led Sir Charles Maxwell to state: 'I never heard a man cursed to my perfect satisfaction until I heard [the adjutant] anathematised in the Phoenix Park.' P.W. Joyce.)

Jesus, sweet God and Father of the Lamb
Who sees us in shackles, too harshly bound,
Since you made us Christians from Friday till Monday

morning
Shelter us and dismiss this scum from us.
(From the Irish. Spoken against British soldiers.)

Like the Clonmacnoise mason, may you never finish what
you set out to do.
(A reference to the unfinished round-tower of Clonmacnoise.)

It was Dermot Rua O'Rahilly
Who cast the books into the sea:
May the red demons hoist him
Away up into the sky ...
God's curse and His Church's
Be on that hateful rock,
Which sank the ship
Without fury of the storm,
Without a wind or gale.
(Michael Kirby, quoting from Tomas Rua's 'The Song of the Books'.)

Hurroo, minister who paid me tuppence
After keening your child
His violent death be on the rest of them
Back to the very end.

The town of Naas is an awful place,
Kilcock is just as bad;
But of all the places I've ever been
Well curse (or worse expletive) you Kinnegad.

Damn the cardboard shields the Dominicans used in Spain,
those bloodstained bowsies.
(Flann O'Brien.)

Curses, like chickens, come home to roost
And if you say 'Up Dev!' may you be clockin'!

Vote for pauper, vote for toff;
If you vote for the Blueshirts, may your hand fall off.

Tara will be forlorn, Skreen will never be without a rogue.
(Said to have been uttered by St Patrick.)

The curse of Cromwell on you.
(Which was: 'To hell or to Connaught!')

The curse of the twelve Biddies on you.

May your children sweep Colmcille's bed against you.

My curse on Straid; may there never be more than one
couple from one townsland married there.
(Said to have been uttered by Colmcille.)

My curse on you and Crossconnel and may it never be
without a fool.
(Ditto.)

The curse of the Cassidys on you.
*(Placed on the distilling family from Monasterevin by a Fr Prendergast
who was hanged in 1798. They had power to request one reprieve each
year but refused to do so in his case.)*

Evil death, short life to Caeir!
May spears of battle destroy Caeir!
May Caeir perish! May Caeir pay! May it reach Caeir!
Under rocks and mounds may Caeir be!
*(Caeir was a supposed pre-Christian Connaught king. Translation from
the Irish by Patrick C. Power.)*

May hound-wounding, heart-ache, and vultures gouging

her eyes,
Derangement and madness on her mind come soon!
May entrails and mansion of pleasure out of the worm fall
  out!
But may she still be alive till everyone's sick at the sight ...
Rain and fire; illwind and snow and hard frost follow her!
May Aeolus chase her into the harbours of Acheron down!
Nine times sicker than the Ulstermen's illness let her be!
May this insect get an illness that Hippocrates cannot cure.
(From Peadar Ó Doirín's poem An Guairne *which expresses anger at
being betrayed in love. Translation by Patrick C. Power.)*

I call on you, oh stone,
To keep Breed below.
She kept us short of drink
And on our house brought shame.
And since, oh Breed, you're buried now,
Eternal thirst to you and drought.
*(Uttered by the poet, Raftery at the grave of a mean housekeeper.
Translated by Patrick C. Power.)*

Bad luck to the people of Kerry
Bad luck to the men of Kildare
But the luck of the devil from hell
On the landlord O'Brien from Clare.

Major Sirr, despised cur ,
The Chief of Dublin's peelers,
May Satan be your guest for tea
And all his evil dealers.

My curse attend Dungarvan,
Her boats, her borough and her fish!
May every woe that mars man,
Come dancing down upon her dish!

For all the thieves behind you,

From Slaney's banks to Shannon side,
Are poor scholars, mind you!
To the rogues you'd meet in Abbeyside.
(Uttered by a blind beggar robbed in Abbeyside, Dungarvan. Padraic Colum.)

Curses from Poets and Writers

May fire and brimstone never fail
To fall in showers on Doneraile;
May all the leading friends assail
The thieving town of Doneraile.

As lightnings flash across the vale
So down to hell with Doneraile;
The fate of Pompey at Pharsale,
Be that the curse of Doneraile.

May beef or mutton, lamb or veal,
Be never found in Doneraile;
But garlic soup, and scurvy kale,
Be still the food of Doneraile.

And forward as the creeping snail,
Th' industry be of Doneraile;
May Heav'n a chosen curse entail
On rigid, rotten Doneraile.

May sun and moon forever fail
To beam their lights in Doneraile;
May every pestilential gale
Blast that cursed spot called Doneraile.

May no sweet cuckoo, thrush or quail,
Be ever heard in Doneraile;
May patriots, kings and commonweal,
Despise and harass Doneraile.

May every Post, Gazette and Mail
Sad tidings bring of Doneraile;
May loudest thunders ring a peal,
To blind and deafen Doneraile.

May vengeance fall at head and tail,
From north to south, at Doneraile;
May profit light and tardy sale
Still damp the trade of Doneraile.

May fame resound a dismal tale,
When e'er she lights on Doneraile;
May Egypt's plagues at once prevail,
To thin the knaves of Doneraile.

May frost and snow and sleet and hail,
Benumb each joint in Doneraile;
May wolves and bloodhounds trace and trail
The cursed crew of Doneraile.

May Oscar, with his fiery flail,
To atoms thresh all Doneraile;
May every mischief, fresh and stale,
Abide, henceforth in Doneraile.

May all, from Belfast to Kinsale,
Scoff, curse and damn you, Doneraile;
May neither flour nor oatenmeal
Be found or known in Doneraile.

May want and woe each joy curtail
That e'er was known in Doneraile;
May no one coffin want a nail
That wraps a rogue in Doneraile.

May all the thieves that rob and steal,
The gallows meet in Doneraile;
May all the sons of Grainewail
Blush at the thieves of Doneraile.

May mischief, big as Norway's whale,
O'erwhelm the knaves of Doneraile;
May curses, wholesale and retail,
Pour with full force on Doneraile.

May every transport wont to sail
A convict bring from Doneraile;
May every churn and milking pail
Fall dry to staves in Doneraile.

May cold and hunger still congeal
The stagnant blood of Doneraile;
May every hour new woes reveal,
That hell reserves for Doneraile.

May every chosen ill prevail
O'er all the imps of Doneraile;
May no one wish or prayers avail
To soothe the woes of Doneraile.

May th' Inquisition straight impale
The rapparees of Doneraile;
May Charon's boat triumphant sail,
Completely manned, from Doneraile.

Oh, may my couplets never fail
To find a curse for Doneraile;
And may grim Pluto's inner sail
Forever groan with Doneraile.
(Patrick 'The Poet' O'Kelly. From James N. Healy.)

Lord, confound this surly sister,
Blight her brow with blotch and blister,
Cramp her larynx, lung, and liver,
In her guts a galling give her.
Let her live to earn her dinners
In Mountjoy with seedy sinners:
Lord, this judgement quickly bring,
And I'm Your servant, J. M. Synge.
(J. M. Synge, 'The Curse'. To a sister of an enemy of Synge's who dis-
approved of his play, The Playboy of the Western World.)

Take our eyes, but leave us men,

Alive or dead
Sons of Wattin!
Sing the vengeance of the Welshmen of Tirawley.
(Samuel Ferguson, 'The Forging of the Anchor'.)

Grief on you, Morris!
Heart's blood and bowels' blood!
May your eyes go blind
And your knees be broken! ...
Destruction pursue you,
Morris the traitor,
Who brought death to my husband!
Father of three children
Two on the hearth
And one in the womb
That I will not bring forth.
(Eileen O'Leary, 'The Lament for Art Ó Laoghaire', Eighteenth Century.)

God rot him and his children.
(Ibid.)

Death to every foe and traitor!
Forward! strike the marching tune ...
(John Keegan Casey, 'The Rising of the Moon'.)

Woe to the miners for Truth – where the Lampless have mined!
Woe to the seekers on earth for – what none ever find!
(James Clarence Mangan, 'Gone in the Wind'.)

Woe is me! by fraud and wrong –
Traitors false and tyrants strong –
Fell Clan Usnach, bought and sold
For Barach's feast and Conor's gold!

Woe to Eman, roof and wall! –
Woe to Red Branch, hearth and hall! –
Tenfold woe and black dishonour
To the false and foul Clan Conor!
(Samuel Ferguson, 'Deirdre's Lament for the Sons of Usnach'.)

May nothing good come to them
But slaughter and terror
Until they are spent.
Nor halt or adjustment assist;
May no rock, hill or mountain offer shelter;
That their lives may be like the hunted fox or game.
(From the Irish, Máire Bhuí Ní Láoire, 'Cath Cheím an Fhía'.)

Searing mountains and scalding heart
Curse that place of drowning.
For its many the creature it has left in woe
Thinking and mourning each Monday morning.
(From the Irish. Antoine Ó Reachtabhra, 'Anach Cúain'.)

My grief on the sea, 'tis it that's huge
Swelling twixt me and my darling.
(Anon. From the Irish, 'Mo Bhrón ar an bhFarraige'.)

Oh I curse the stifling, smothering breath of the religion that
withered my loving and my living and my womanhood.
(John B. Keane, Big Maggie, Finale.)

All blessings from heaven to earth
On the head of the woman I hate,
And the man I love as my life,
Sudden death be his fate.
(Frank O'Connor, Trans. 'A Learned Mistress'.)

More Curses for Special Occasions

That your arm may get twisted as a bog blackthorn.
(Uttered by wrestlers at hurling matches long ago.)

If she turns first may she take the road to hell.
(Said at coursing matches.)

May the sun get shy before he finishes.
(Said when an enemy is about to go haymaking.)

Bad scran to those who pay the priest more heed than their neighbours.
(Example of imprecation when religion was placed before vital help.)

Be the Dhalum seek sudil but I'll corib your jeel.
(Tinker's cant: By the good God Almighty, I will kill you tonight.)

Tasp gut may luber you.
(Tinkers' cant: The curse of God on you.)

The Lord look down on the crackawly who did it.
(Uttered after some destruction is done by a stupid person in Cork.)

That he may carry his traps in his trews.
(Cork slang. May he carry all his belongings in his trouser pockets. Said in ill-will, especially if buying a drink is shirked.)

May hell's heat dry his lips, the mean mank.
(Said when a dirty fellow [mank] dodges buying his round of drinks.)

Blast the divil that brought you this way.
(Said to an unwelcome stranger.)

That it may choke you a mile from a well.
(Said to someone who is eating or drinking but who does not offer hospitality.)

Amusing Imprecations

May the devil catch you and take you to where you cannot be found.

May he be shot by a bullet or smothered in bed hungry.

May the man who steals my flute lose the power of his limbs and never blow even soup.

May you be gummy by the time you have mate on your table.

May the devil's dowser dip his twig to your buttermilk.

That Cromwell's corpse may rise again and give you good looks.

Cold wife;
Long life;
Short grass;
Small glass;
Empty grate;
Wee plate;
And curse o' God on you too, you whore's melt!

Forty weasels chew your lights,
Perforate your bowels with bites
Till you're leaking like a collander of gruel.
May a ferret with a grin,
Lash its molars to your chin
As you scream in pain like Festy Flynn, the fool.

Curse the man who twists his lips
When with you hot punch he sips;
Curse him twice if bread he breaks
Gosthering on like Kelly's drakes.
Curse him if you see him scratch
When you take him 'neath your thatch;
For the shifty, grey-faced swine
Will be gone at half-past-nine.
Curse him every day you 'waken
For your woman he'll have taken.

May your heifer never get to the bull.

May you be torn in strips and have a rag for a bonnet.

Your skeleton and its two sons rout you.

May muck-maggots gulp your guts,
Chew your fingers to the butts
Crawling in and out your navel, night and day;
And a hundred swarms of bees
Lodge two feet above your knees,
'Cause you tumbled holy women in the hay.

That you may spend your days burning tarred rope in a
bucket and squatting on it.
(Regarded as a cure for piles.)

May a consumptive cobbler castrate you on a red-hot last.

The pus of a poxy fox in your whiskey.

That you may be left a hundred pounds and the will lost.

May you starve till you can kiss a goat between the horns.

May there be only a cripple around to get the priest for you.

Death and bad luck afterwards to you.

May you croak, confound you, and may you get the pip.
(*A disease in fowl.*)

The devil go with you and sixpence and then you'll never want for company or money.

Six eggs to you and a half-dozen of them rotten.

May your last hornpipe be in the air.
(*May you hang.*)

That you may melt off the earth like snow off a ditch and may there be a river of fire to catch you.

Die and give the hungry crow a black-pudding.

Don't starve the scald-crows – die in a ditch next winter.

Here's my gift for you:
    A useless, useful instrument;
    Bought for money, it cannot be lent.
    Although you now own it, it isn't your own
    But I hope that it soon will carry you home.
(*It is a coffin.*)

May you suffer everything that Cromwell might give except his money.

May you have nothing in your bag at the going down of the sun and less when it rises.

Before you enter heaven, may St Peter demand that you light a fire on a lake or advise a headstrong woman.

That you may wear out more sheets than soles.

That the only full pockets you'll ever have be in your habit.

A curse on your house if you have one; if you haven't, blast the stars.

May the Lord call you when your master is away and his larder full.

That your feet may have blisters when they're dancing the angel's hornpipe.

Well wear, soon tear
Then you can give the ragman his share.

May his pipe never smoke, may his tay-pot be broke,
And to add to the joke may his kettle ne'er boil.
May he stick to his bed till the hour that he's dead,
May he always be fed on hog's wash and boiled oil.
May he swell with the gout, may his grinders fall out
May he roll, howl and shout with the horrid toothache –
May the temples wear horns and the toes many corns
Of the monster that murdered Ned Flaherty's drake!

May his dog yelp and howl with the hunger and cold,
May his wife ever scold till his hair it turns grey;

May the curse of each hag that e'er carried a bag
Alight on his head 'till his hair it turns grey.
May every oul' fairy from Cork to Dun Laoghaire
Duck him snug and airy in river and lake.
May the plague take the scamp; that the divil may stamp
On the monster that murdered Ned Flaherty's drake.

May his pig never grunt, may his cat never hunt,
May a ghost ever haunt him at dead of the night!
May his hen never lay, may his ass never bray;
May his goat fly away like an old paper kite.
That witches affright him; that mad dogs may bite him,
And every one slight him asleep or awake
Bad wind to the robber be he drunk or sober,
The monster that murdered Ned Flaherty's drake!

(James N. Healy's version of an old recitation.)

Bad luck to this marching,
Pipeclaying and starching,
How neat one must be
To be killed by the French!

(Charles J. Lever, 'Bad Luck to this Marching'.)

When the last train leaves for heaven may you still be in the waiting-room.

May your soul's transport be a lame jinnet with diarrhoea that's also fond of the fire.

When it rains gold, may you be without a spoon.

Coarse, Profane and Mixed

Shag me, said the duchess, more in hope than in anger.

St Patrick's curse on Ardagh to you: never without a liar, a rogue and a whore.

My blessing on you but my curse on your uncivil tongue.

Blast you from a height.

Shag you, you whore's melt.

That you may marry the town bicycle.

Blast you to hell, you poxy go-by-the-road.

May your obituary be written in weasel's piss.

The curse of Jesus Christ on a whore-house on you.

That you may shit sideways.

May the devil swallow you sideways and choke on your pecker.

May the lamb of God stir his hoof through the roof of heaven and kick you in the arse down to hell.
(John M. Feehan.)

May the devil cut your genitals out and feed them to the pigs.
(Ibid.)

Be the twenty-four balls of the twelve apostles.
(Ibid.)

The devil roast the balls off you and skewer them.

Be the scurvy spittle of a drunken hoor!

That the skin of your pecker may fester.

That you may ride the divil's wife and she with glass inside her.

> May Old Nick's balls bounce on your bed,
> His spittle stain your pillow.
> And may you ever sleep in dread
> Of his big, black, wobbly willow.

May your daughter's only job be making beds in a kip-house.

That you may marry a get who would be a bastard even if his parents married.

> Feck this house, O Lord, we pray,
> Feck it for its watery tay [tea].
> Feck the 'guvnor' – whining shite,
> Letting in mad dogs to fight.
> Feck the roof, that it may fall
> Upon the res'dents, one and all.

Feck the door that it may be
Ever open to escapees.
(Parody on 'Bless this House', favoured by convicts.)

A landlord's pox on you and yours.

May you get a witch's syphilis from your broom-handle!

1. That your arse may close up.
2. Yours cannot, for you're always talking through it.

Wherever you go, may you be as welcome as a fart in a telephone kiosk.

May your woman be frigid, your Ned knotted and may you be filled with bad thoughts.

That you may burst, you hungry hoor!

When she gave it to you
She gave it to others;
May she give to you
What she gave to others.
When she gave it to others,
She has it.
If she has, may you get it.
If you get it, you get,
Then bejaysus – You've had it.
And so be it, you git!

A curse on Parnell and Tim Healy as well
On Members of Parliament, snooty and swell;
A curse on Dick Pigott, who told of the vice
Between Kitty O'Shea and the leader of lice.

May Avondale's blackbird, lose pecker and bone
Be they crushed 'neath the weight of decrepit Gladstone.

Blast you for a tinker; may you be wandering hungry till your ankles wear up to your balls; and may your mangy dog eat what's left and leave you with rabies as well.

May the buggers live to be very old and any that would not live to be that age may they die young.

Be the lamb of the lantern lord jaysus!

Be the livin' jinnets!

Bedamned for saying 'God Bless us!'; sudden prayer makes God jump.

Blast the slimy, two-faced get; he's so far up my arse I can taste him.

May the divil gulp you so far down his throat that you'll have to shove your toothbrush up his arse to clean your teeth.

May the devil put his hoof far up your arse and drag the ferrule of your hole below your knee!

With all your money, airs and graces, may you be left where the crows don't shite.

May the hairs on your arse turn into drumsticks and beat the shite out of you.

(After my final visit to the Department of Folklore in University College Dublin, I had occasion to visit a student's lavatory. I noticed the following piece of graffiti there:)

May your pubes go up in flames and your balls burn.

(The future of the coarse curse is in safe hands!)

Bibliography

Journals and Manuscripts

Béaloideas, The Journal of the Folklore Society of Ireland, Vols 1 to 49.
Irish Folklore Collection – Mss. The Department of Irish Folklore, University College, Dublin.
Author's personal manuscript collection.

Books

Barrington, Sir Jonah, *Personal Sketches of his own Times*, Vol 1 (London 1830).
Brontës, *The Poems of Emily Jane Brontë and Anne Brontë*, eds Wise/Symington (Oxford 1934).
Carney, James, *Medieval Irish Lyrics with the Irish Bardic Poet* (Mountrath 1985).
Clancy, Eileen and Patrick Forde, *Ballinagleara Parish* (Dublin 1980).
Colum, Padraic (ed), *Broadsheet Ballads* , Chosen and with an Introduction by Padraic Colum (Dublin 1913).
Colum, Padraic, *A Treasury of Irish Folklore* (New York 1967).
Corry, T C, *Irish Lyrics, Songs and Poems* (Belfast 1879).
de h-Íde, Dubhglas, *Amhain Chúige Chonnacht: An Leath Rann* (Baile Átha Cliath 1922).
Egan, Desmond, *A Song for my Father* (Newbridge 1989).
Feehan, John, *My Village – My World* (Cork and Dublin 1992).
Graves, A P, *Songs of Killarney* , London (1873).
Gregory, Lady, *The Blessed Trinity of Ireland* (Gerrards Cross 1985).
Healy, James N, *Comic Irish Recitations* (Cork and Dublin 1981).
Henry, P L, *Dánta Ban* (Cork and Dublin 1991).
Hyde, Douglas, *The Religious Songs of Connaught, Vol 2* (Dublin and London 1922).
Joyce, James, *Ulysses* (London 1936).
Joyce, P W, *English as we Speak it* (Dublin 1979).
Keane, John B, *Three Plays* (Cork and Dublin 1990).
Kearney, Peadar, *Down by the Glenside* (Dublin 1966).
Kennelly, Brendan, *Moloney up and at it* (Cork and Dublin 1984).
Kennelly, Brendan (ed), *The Penguin Book of Irish Verse* (London 1970).
Kirby, Michael, *Skelligside* (Dublin 1990).
Leyden, Maurice (ed), *Belfast – City of Song* (Dingle 1989).
McGuffin, John, *In Praise of Poteen* (Belfast 1978).

McMahon, Seán (ed), *A Book of Irish Quotations* (Dublin 1984).

McMahon, Seán, *Rich and Rare* (Co. Dublin 1984).

McMahon, Seán and O'Donoghue, Jo (ed), *Taisce Duain* (Co. Dublin 1992).

Moore, Thomas, *The Poetical Works of Thomas Moore* (Philadelphia 1836).

O'Brien, Edna, *Some Irish Loving* (London 1981).

O'Brien, Flann, *The Hard Life* (Dublin 1961).

Ó Buachalla, Séamus, *The Literary Writings of Patrick Pearse* (Cork and Dublin 1982).

Ó Catháin, Séamas, *Irish Life and Lore* (Cork and Dublin 1982).

O'Casey, Seán, *Collected Plays* (London 1949).

Ó Donnchú, M F, *Leo* (Baile Átha Clíath 1981).

O'Donnell, Patrick, *The Irish Faction Fighters of the Nineteenth Century* (Dublin 1975).

O'Farrell, Padraic, *How the Irish Speak English* (Cork and Dublin 1980).

O'Farrell, Padraic, *Gems of Irish Wisdom – Proverbs and Sayings* (Cork and Dublin 1980).

Ó Muimhneacháin, Aindrias, *Stories from The Tailor* (Cork and Dublin, undated).

Ó Súilleabháin, Seán, *A Handbook of Irish Folklore* (Dublin 1942).

O'Sullivan, Seán, *The Folklore of Ireland* (London 1974).

Ó Tuama, Seán, (Trans Kinsella, Thomas), *An Duanaire 1600-1900: Poems of the Dispossessed* (Mountrath 1981).

Power, Patrick C, *The Book of Irish Curses* (Cork and Dublin 1974).

Smith, Sydney Bernard, *Scurrilities* (Dublin 1981).

Synge, John M, *Plays, Poems and Prose* (London 1941).

Swift, Jonathan, *The Author's Works Vols 1 to 6* (Dublin 1763).

Wilde, Lady, *Ancient Charms and Superstitions of Ireland* (London 1925).

Wilde, Sir William, *Irish Popular Superstitions* (Dublin 1852).

Yeats, William B, *Collected Poems* (London 1919).

Yeats, William B, *The Illustrated Poets* (London 1990).

Acknowledgements

I wish to thank Professor Bo Almquist, Director of the Department of Irish Folklore, University College, Dublin and the Editor of *Béaloideas* for allowing me to translate and use direct quotes from manuscripts and published material. I thank also their staffs, especially Bairbre Ó Floinn and Dr Séamas Ó Catháin. Séamas also kindly allowed me to quote at length from his book *Irish Life and Lore* (Cork and Dublin 1982). I am indebted too to the other authors credited in the text, or their representatives, for use of material. I thank the following publishers for use of quotations from their publications:

Anvil Books, Dublin; Raven Arts Press; B T Batsford Ltd, Irish Academic Press, Dublin; Colin Smythe, Gerrards Cross; The Lilliput Press, Dublin; Mercier Press, Cork and Dublin; The Kavanagh Press, Newbridge; Methuen, London; O'Brien Press, Dublin; Penguin Books, London; Poolbeg Press, Co. Dublin; Walton's, Dublin; Harper/Collins (Grafton), London; Faber and Faber, London (*The Collected Poems of Louis McNeice*, Ed E R Dodds); MLR Agency (Patricia MacNaughton), London and the Estate of Sean O'Casey. I thank the Estate of Padraic Colum for quotation from *Broadsheet Ballads*: Chosen with an Introduction by Padraic Colum; the Frank O'Connor Estate and Séan Nicholson.

Thanks to the librarian and staff of the National Library, Trinity College Library and Westmeath County Library.

Once again, I thank the editor and staff of the Mercier Press; my wife, Maureen, for efficient proof-reading and my family for continuing patience. *Beannacht Dé Oraibh!*

The abbreviation IFC Ms refers to manuscripts in the Irish Folklore Collection, Department of Irish Folklore, University College Dublin. 'From the Irish', without further qualification, denotes my own translation of old writings in the Irish language. Uncredited entries are from my own manuscript sources, compiled over a long number of years.

Padraic O'Farrell

SUPERSTITIONS OF IRISH COUNTRY PEOPLE

Padraic O'Farrell

Do you know why it is considered unlucky to meet a bare-footed man, to start a journey on the tenth of November, to get married on a Saturday?

Irish country people believe that angels are always present among them and that all good things – crops, rain and so forth come from them. Bad spirits bring sickness to humans, animals and pestilence to crops. They do not speak of fairies on Wednesdays and Fridays for on those days *they* could be present while still being invisible.

GEMS OF IRISH WISDOM:
IRISH PROVERBS AND SAYINGS

Padraic O'Farrell

Gems of Irish Wisdom is a fascinating collection of Irish proverbs and sayings.

The tallest flowers hide the strongest nettles.
The man who asks what good is money has already paid for his plot.
A man begins cutting his wisdom teeth the first time he bites off more than he can chew.
Even if you are on the right track, you'll be run over if you stay there.
The road to heaven is well signposted but badly lit at night.
Love is like stirabout, it must be made fresh every day.

A History of Irish Fairies

Carolyn White

Whether you believe in fairies or not you cannot ignore them and here for the first time is *A History of Irish Fairies*. Having no stories directly from the fairies themselves, we must rely on descriptions by mortal men and women. A large part of this book is concerned with the relations between mortals and fairies, so that the reader may determine the best way to behave whenever he encounters fairies. The book contains such interesting details as the distinction and confusion between cluricaun and leprechaun and the fact that only male infants are stolen from the cradle. You can read about the Far Darrig, Merrows and Silkies, Banshees and Keening, the Lianhan Shee, Pookas, Dullahans and Ghosts.

In *A History of Irish Fairies* we find all the magic of the 'wee people'. The author deals with their important place in country folklore and tells us of their mannerisms, clothing, food and love-life.

Folktales of the Irish Countryside

Kevin Danaher

Nowadays there is a whole generation growing up who cannot remember a time when there was no television; and whose parents cannot remember a time when there was no radio and cinema. It is not, therefore, surprising that many of them wonder what people in country places found to do with their time in winters of long ago. People may blink in astonishment when reminded of the fact that the night was often too short for those past generations of country people, whose own entertainment with singing, music, dancing, cards, indoor games, and story-telling spanned the evenings and into morning light.

Kevin Danaher remembers forty of the stories that enlivened those past days. Some are stories told by members of his own family; others he took down in his own countryside from the last of the tradi-tional storytellers. Included are stories of giants, of ghosts, of wondrous deeds, queer happenings, of the fairies and the great kings of Ireland who had beautiful daughters and many problems.

A homely, heartwarming collection of tales that spring naturally from the heart of the Irish countryside.

The Irish Cookbook

Carla Blake

The Irish Cookbook fills a long felt need for the young Irishwoman and every woman who would like to add to her culinary skills and try cooking Irish style.

Traditional Irish dishes are slightly adapted to suit present day tastes and methods and included are some modern Irish recipes using Guinness, Irish Whiskey, Irish Hams and Irish Cheese.

All the basic methods for making soup and cooking fish, meat and vegetables are given with a selection of unusual recipes. Suggestions are also made about accompaniments to make a pleasantly balanced meal. There are recipes to see you through all occasions from family meals and 'Quick and Easy' snacks to dinner parties.

Writing simply and clearly the author avoids the use of French culinary terms which often confuse the inexperienced cook. Recipes are given in ounces and grammes.

TOSS THE FEATHERS
IRISH SET DANCING

PAT MURPHY

Toss the Feathers provides a comprehensive approach to set dancing. It contains sixty-four complete set dances, including all those danced commonly in classes, summer schools and at feiseanna. These are laid out in conventional set terminology and can be easily followed by teachers, pupils and anyone who has an acquaintance with the art of set dancing. The book also contains the first concise history of the development of set dancing in Ireland from its eighteenth-century European origins.

IN MY FATHER'S TIME

EAMON KELLY

In My Father's Time invites us to a night of storytelling by Ireland's greatest and best loved seanchaí, Eamon Kelly. The fascinating stories reveal many aspects of Irish life and character. There are tales of country customs, matchmaking, courting, love, marriage and the dowry system, emigration, American wakes and returned emigrants. The stream of anecdotes never runs dry and the humour sparkles and illuminates the stories.

IRELAND IN LOVE

Selected by ANTHONY BLUETT

Ireland in Love is a lively collection of some of the country's most striking and unusual love traditions.

Did you know, for instance, that purple orchids were used in 'coaxing' women in Kerry and white gander droppings were employed to secure the love of a man in Cork?

The book brings together a variety of original texts which offer advice, help or simply amusement on such questions as telling the future, casting charms, laying curses and of course, matchmaking. This collection also contains a selection of songs, sayings, quotations and poems, including an excerpt from the outrageous *Midnight Court*.

DICTIONARY OF IRISH QUOTATIONS

SEAN SHEEHAN

Dictionary of Irish Quotations contains a highly enjoyable and varied selection of interesting, informative, intriguing, infuriating – and sometimes just witty – remarks made by Irish people on a number of topical subjects. The quotations included range from the fifth century to today and from the classical to the colloquial. There are over 150 authors from St Brigid to Sinéad O'Connor. Yeats and Swift are quoted here and Wilde and Joyce. So too are Maria Edgeworth and Mary Lavin; Robert Emmet and Roger Casement; Douglas Hyde and Mary Robinson; Sean Hughes and Neil Jordan ...

THINGS IRISH

ANTHONY BLUETT

Things Irish provides the reader with an entertaining and informative view of Ireland, seen through the practices, beliefs and everyday objects that seem to belong specifically to this country. Discarding the usual format of chapters on a variety of themes, the book uses short descriptive passages on anything from whiskey to standing stones, from May Day to hurling, in order to create a distinctive image of Irish life. The reader is free to roam from topic to topic, from passage to passage, discovering a wealth of new and surprising facts and having a number of misguided beliefs put right.

THE GREAT IRISH FAMINE

EDITED BY CATHAL PÓIRTÉIR

This is the most wide-ranging series of essays ever published on the Great Irish Famine and will prove of lasting interest to the general reader. Leading historians, economists, geographers – from Ireland, Britain and the United States – have assembled the most up-to-date research from a wide spectrum of disciplines, including medicine, folklore and literature, to give the fullest account yet of the background and consequences of the Famine.

Irish Blessings, Toasts and Traditions

Edited by Jason S. Roberts

Often it is said that the Irish are born with the gift of the blarney – and an Irishman can certainly tell a tale like no other. In the rich tradition of Irish lore and legend, tales of fairies with magical powers are the most common as well as the most enjoyable, for when fairies are present there is always the possibility of great fortune or unwitting disaster, not to mention a good story.

This delightful collection brings together the luck and charm of the Irish in a single volume filled with blessings, toasts, old-fashioned customs, sayings, superstitions, jokes, limericks and legends.

You'll find common remedies for simple ailments such as headache, heartache or freckles – and love spells using herbs and poetry such as:

Moon, moon tell unto me,
When my true love I shall see?

What fine clothes am I to wear?
How many children will I bear?

For if my love comes not to me,
Dark and dismal my life will be.

From the wailing and the clapping of the Banshee to the dancing and whimsical pranks of the Little People, here are gems of Irish folklore and tradition guaranteed to enchant old and young alike.